GLASGOW RAILWAY MEMORIES

By
W.A.C. Smith
and Paul Anderson

Copyright IRWELL PRESS
ISBN 1-903266-09-2

First published in the United Kingdom in 2001
by Irwell Press Ltd.,
59A, High Street, Clophill,
Bedfordshire MK45 4BE
Printed and bound by Interprint, Malta

CONTENTS

ACKNOWLEDGEMENTS

While compiling this book, our sixth joint project, W.A.C. Smith and Paul Anderson received valuable help from others. In this instance, Doris deserves a special accolade. Apart from the customary encouragement, patience and proof reading, she made a contribution in the form of memories of Corkerhill Railway Village. Juliet Whitworth of Barrow upon Soar did the drawings, Pip Bloor of Thurmaston provided the shed allocations and Ken MacKay supplied the unique photograph of the Royal Scot on Coronation Day. Many thanks from the authors in Glasgow and Leicester respectively.

A memorable picture to begin this series of memories of Glasgow's railways. In pouring rain, V3 2-6-2T No.67618 awaits departure from Airdrie with the 5.18pm to Anniesland on 1st April 1961. Perhaps this atmospheric scene was not fully appreciated by the three young ladies bound for a Saturday night on the town, especially as steam had temporarily replaced the electric 'Blue Train' service.

CHAPTER 1
OBSERVATIONS

For over a century, the railway press has reported the allocation and movements of locomotives, the sighting of unusual workings and the influx of 'foreign' engines on special occasions. But the day to day running of trains has received far less coverage, and that includes those amusing or irritating incidents which everyone can recall, yet hardly anybody can be precise about. During the 1940s it was a case of bearing up during wartime conditions, then coping with the austerity that followed. In the 1950s trains were taken for granted, whether the journey involved work, business, recreation or holidays. Then came the upheaval of the 1960s, when changes in society, an upsurge in car ownership, and Beeching's pruning of the system made the railways, frankly, unfashionable. Throughout these three decades, there was a particularly noticeable lack of interest in Scotland. Even the poignant end of 136 years of steam traction in Glasgow, a force which had played a major part in creating this great industrial city, was marked by general apathy amongst railway employees, passengers and even enthusiasts.

Fortunately, W.A.C. Smith was fascinated by railways and locomotives from a very early age. He decided to make notes on passing trains and actual journeys in 1941 and has been doing so ever since. His observations from the steam era are now an invaluable record of a vanished way of life, for they are not merely comments on 'practice and performance', but an insight into many different aspects of train travel – and, for that matter, society in general. The activity at stations and sheds, the effects of severe weather, the work required of railway staff and the odd occasion when something went really wrong, all appear in the following pages. The stories are very much a personal selection and no attempt has been made to cover Glasgow's complex railway system comprehensively.

Over the last half century, there have been immense changes in virtually every aspect of everyday life. Television and telephones were around in the early 1950s, but satellite TV and mobiles would have seemed literally fantastic then. Any thoughts of computer screens rather than ledgers on nearly every office desk, let alone the Internet, would similarly have inhabited the realms of science fiction. The virtual annihilation of coal mining and heavy engineering was hardly envisaged, neither was the phenomenal growth of road traffic and air travel. However, a few long established institutions have survived and in some cases flourished. Along with radio – the wireless – and real ale, railways have enjoyed a revival. Glasgow's trains are very different to those of five decades ago, but they still play a vital role in running the rejuvenated city. The authors hope that those who use them or know them today will find these glimpses of the past an interesting and amusing contrast to the scene at the beginning of the millennium.

Apart from a very brief summary at the beginning of each chapter, historical information about the system has been omitted. For further details, readers are advised to consult *An Illustrated History of Glasgow's Railways* by W.A.C. Smith and Paul Anderson, published by Irwell Press in 1993. That work also includes comprehensive maps and a wide range of photographs.

A busy summer Saturday morning, 29th June 1957, at West Street Junction on the goods line from Larkfield Junction to Shields Junction, which connected the Rutherglen and Paisley routes. The view was taken from the bridge carrying the Cathcart Circle and Barrhead lines. Standard 5MT No.73010 comes through on the 9.25am Heads of Ayr to Edinburgh Princes Street while Black Five No.44886 on a Clyde Coast relief from Lanarkshire coalfield stations takes water and changes crews. Caley 'Jumbo' No.57278 stands in the loop at the mineral depot with a freight. Sidings on the course of the early Polloc & Govan Railway are on the right.

Ex-North British J37 0-6-0 No.64563 from Parkhead shed ambles through Ibrox station with a coast-bound Sunday School trip on 28th May 1955. The train consists mainly of former LMS non-corridor stock, although the leading vehicle is of North Eastern origin. It started at a north side suburban station and travelled via the City Union line between High Street East Junction and Pollok Junction to reach the Paisley Joint route. Ibrox station, surprising in view of its proximity to the Glasgow Rangers stadium, closed when the line was electrified and reduced to double track.

A touch of opulence at Glasgow's least opulent terminus. Pullman cars appeared on the Caledonian Railway in 1914 and more of these luxurious vehicles were introduced following World War I, but when the agreement with the Pullman Car Company expired in 1933 they were taken into LMS stock. The coaches received that company's maroon livery and remained in service on the Oban and Far North lines well into BR days. At Buchanan Street station on 1st August 1959, SC219M (built in 1927 and originally named QUEEN MARGARET) is being removed from the 11.45am Oban-Glasgow by Fairburn 2-6-4T No.42207, prior to its return working at 5.15pm.

With expresses from Central, Queen Street and St Enoch, trains to the Highlands from Buchanan Street and an endless procession of suburban services throughout the city, it is easy to forget the fact that the lifeblood of Glasgow's railways was originally goods. Standard Mogul No.76103 climbs briskly past Sighthill East Junction with a freight from Buchanan Street Goods on 18th March 1961, sadly at a time when road transport was beginning to make a real impact on such traffic.

At 18.15 on the evening of Friday 28th April 1967, the curtain comes down on 136 years of Scottish steam as Fairburn 2-6-4T No.42274 propels the empty stock of the 17.03 from Gourock out of platform 12 at Glasgow Central towards Smithy Lye sidings. The ten remaining weekday steam turns were then taken over by diesel multiple units. Complete dieselisation of the Gourock service was short-lived, new electric Blue Trains similar to that on the left being introduced later in the year.

Although Stanier 5MT 4-6-0s, joined later by the BR Standard version, were the staple diet at Buchanan Street during the first fourteen years of nationalisation, the scene changed dramatically in 1962 when there was an influx of LNER designs. On 31st August 1965, during the twilight of steam, A4 Pacific No.60026 MILES BEEVOR heads the 5.30pm 'Saint Mungo' three hour express for Aberdeen and B1 4-6-0 No.61244 STRANG STEEL waits with the 5.35pm to Dunblane.

'Steam for Ever' reads the chalked slogan on the buffer beam of A4 Pacific No.60007 SIR NIGEL GRESLEY, making a spirited departure from Buchanan Street with the 5.30pm 'Saint Mungo' express for Aberdeen on 20th August 1964. A Type 2 diesel is at platform 1 with the 5.50pm to Callander. Buchanan Street closed in 1966 and the site is now partly occupied by Glasgow Caledonian University.

CHAPTER 2
NORTH SIDE

The North Side of Glasgow has always been markedly different in character from other parts of the city. Physically, it is dominated by the western extremity of the Monklands plateau which culminates in a fairly steep slope down to the Clyde. To the north is the Kelvin valley, a natural routeway utilised by the Romans for the western part of the Antonine Wall and much later by the builders of the Forth & Clyde Canal. In fact the physical configuration of the ground meant that all forms of communication – roads, canal and railways – approached in a parallel fashion from the north east. There was less wholesale suburban development compared with other areas of Glasgow, although the inevitable clusters of tenements grew up around existing villages and hamlets. Above all else, once the railways were established the North Side became dominated by locomotive building. Besides the huge works at Cowlairs and St. Rollox, belonging to the North British and Caledonian respectively, the North British Locomotive Company had two mighty plants at Springburn.

Two pioneering railways approached the city from the Monklands plateau.

The Garnkirk & Glasgow opened in 1831, terminating at Townhead near the large Tennant's chemical factory. Although coal and other industrial traffic provided its lifeblood, passenger traffic flourished and an inclined extension down to Buchanan Street in the city centre was opened during 1849 by the line's new owners, the Caledonian Railway. The Edinburgh & Glasgow was Scotland's first trunk line. It opened in 1842 and also featured an incline, in this instance the notorious Cowlairs bank down to Queen Street. Buchanan Street was a ramshackle, almost provincial terminus throughout its life, despite serving some of the most attractive parts of Scotland including places such as Oban, Perth and Aberdeen. Queen Street was also a diabolical station until rebuilt in 1879 with a beautiful arched roof. Nevertheless it remained a smoke-laden cauldron until the end of steam. Both termini were dominated by long distance traffic, with little suburban traffic. The two lines also provided springing points for concentric routes though the north east suburbs.

UP FOR THE CUP

Of Glasgow's four main line termini, Buchanan Street saw the least variety of motive power during the 1950s, although this was to alter drastically in the early 1960s. There were also long periods of inactivity. However, on occasions the station had to be worked to capacity, the Scottish Cup Final between Motherwell and Dundee at Hampden Park on 19th April 1952 being such an instance. No less than 136,000 spectators attended the game. Sixteen specials, all composed of eleven corridors and filled to capacity, ran from Dundee West to the modest five platform

The approach to Buchanan Street station on 27th September 1963, with V2 2-6-2 No.60835 leaving the tunnel from St. Rollox and about to pass under Dobbie's Loan with the 1.30pm ('The Grampian') from Aberdeen. 'Black 5' No.45473, a member of the class which had a virtual monopoly of services during the 1950s, stands in the locomotive siding.

terminus at Buchanan Street. From Motherwell there were six specials to King's Park, and trains ran 'every few minutes' from Glasgow Central to Mount Florida.

Following the match, the first of the Dundee trains was scheduled to leave Buchanan Street at 6.00pm. Long before this, a lengthy queue had formed in a steady downpour of rain, stretching out of the station along Port Dundas Road. Surprisingly enough, the first special (reporting number 115) got away on time from platform 3 with No.44957 (65B St. Rollox), alias Balornock heading eleven Gresley coaches and banked by No.45487 (63A Perth South) which had brought in the empty stock. The next train (112) left from platform 2 at 6.10pm hauled by Balornock's No.44996 (sporting a self-weighing tender). The timetabled 6.10pm for Dundee, carrying the reporting number 113 on this occasion, got away eight minutes late with No.44960 (63A) on three corridors and five non-corridors. Special 110, which loaded at platform 5 normally reserved for parcels traffic, had No.44954 (62B Dundee Tay Bridge) on LNER stock and went out at 6.27pm banked by Fowler 0-6-0 No.44255 (65B) running tender first.

At 6.42pm special 116 left behind No.44797 (63A) banked by No.44969 (65B). It consisted of nine LMS coaches plus two chocolate and cream GWR vehicles. Meanwhile, No.44923 (65B) brought eleven LNER corridors into

platform 3 and this train left at 6.53pm hauled by No.44995 (65B) followed ten minutes later from platform 2 by No.45456 (63A) which had banking assistance from No.45481 (65B). At 7.17pm No.44978 (63A) cleared platform 4 with special 119, consisting of ten LMS corridors plus a GWR vehicle, banked by No.44786 (65B). No.45156 AYRSHIRE YEOMANRY (65B) had brought the stock for special 120 into platform 3 and No.44924 (63A) was at platform 1 with the ordinary 7.35pm to Aberdeen. With *nine* specials still to go, the queue was longer than ever, stretching from the station along Port Dundas Road, into Milton Street and as far as Dobbie's Loan!

UP THE BANK

Queen Street station, in the heart of the city, was undoubtedly the most atmospheric of Glasgow's termini. The ubiquitous bankers simmered at the buffer stops beneath the soot-encrusted arched roof and smoke constantly billowed from the tunnel entrance at the start of the 1¼ mile Cowlairs Incline. It was a station which played host to a variety of splendidly named locomotives, but was always a severe headache for the operating authorities.

My abiding memories are of the great freeze of early 1947, when travelling back to army camp in Edinburgh on Sunday nights by the 9.10pm Colchester train, which loaded to ten corridors and was invariably full. On bleak and

bitterly cold winter nights, shivering passengers packed the cramped concourse as complicated shunting movements took place before a locomotive backed on to the train. The engine could be anything from an LNER Pacific to a North British 4-4-0, but, curiously, never one of the new B1s. Very often, an N15 0-6-2T was attached as pilot instead of banking, the latter duty being entrusted to the main line locomotive which had brought in the stock (on one occasion A4 Pacific No.12 COMMONWEALTH OF AUSTRALIA). Any saving of time on the incline was offset by a stop at Cowlairs to detach the assisting locos. The schedule of 1 hour 21 minutes for the 47¼ miles to Waverley may seem leisurely by present day standards, but there were calls at Falkirk High, Linlithgow and Haymarket, semi-permanent 5/10mph slacks at Bishopbriggs, Lenzie and Linlithgow Viaduct, and coal of indifferent quality because of the fuel crisis. Furthermore, several of the journeys were made in blizzard conditions.

Although seven minutes were allowed from leaving Queen Street to passing Cowlairs West Junction, where the banker normally dropped off by means of its slip coupling, my first run on 19th January was fairly typical of what was to come. Class D49 4-4-0 No.2721 WARWICKSHIRE took eleven minutes to Cowlairs where a stop was necessary to detach A3 Pacific No.43

On 2nd September 1954 the Queen Mother travelled down from Ballater to open the Scottish Industries Exhibition at Kelvin Hall. For the return journey, departure from Buchanan Street station was scheduled for 5.30pm, taking precedence over the ordinary 5.30pm to Dunblane. Immaculate St. Rollox 'Black 5' No.45499 is passing St. Rollox station with the special, made up of five Royal Train vehicles. Standard 5MT No.73005 on the 1.15pm from Aberdeen has been stopped so as not to pass the Royal party in the tunnel.

Garnkirk, in the Monklands coalfield, was the true birthplace of Scotland's railways. Although horse-operated lines already served the district, and the Edinburgh & Dalkeith and Dundee & Newtyle were authorised at the same time as the Garnkirk & Glasgow, the route to St. Rollox and Townhead was, with commendable foresight, the first to embrace the idea of steam traction over double track. Sadly, the significance of the place was totally lost in leaner times 130 years later. On 4th March 1960, Fairburn 2-6-4T No.42196 calls at Garnkirk with the 1.37pm from Gartcosh to Glasgow Buchanan Street. Just two passengers boarded and the station closed the following day.

BROWN JACK which had been banking. The following week, Pacific No.68 SIR VISTO with nine coaches made a good run, while 2nd February was notable, if not for the performance of D49 No.2705 LANARKSHIRE, then for travel in a gas-lit clerestory-roofed saloon! D11 4-4-0s powered my next three runs, the worst of these being on 23rd February with No.2688 ELLEN DOUGLAS. With an N15 as a banker, Cowlairs was passed in a creditable eight minutes, but in heavy snow a series of block failures followed and Waverley was reached half an hour late.

My poorest run was made not with the 9.10pm, but with the 8.30pm relief on 23rd March. It was hauled by D29

Class V2 2-6-2 No.60844 eases into busy Cumbernauld station with the 10.00am Dundee Tay Bridge-Glasgow Buchanan Street on 18th September 1965. The start of the new town can be seen above and beyond the former Caledonian Railway buildings on the left, which have since been replaced by a somewhat featureless brick structure.

Although the ex-LMS Black 5s were partially displaced from their old stamping ground at Buchanan Street during the early 1960s, they had been a familiar sight in former LNER territory just round the corner for some time. On 3rd April 1961 No.44968 stands at Queen Street station with the 10.45am Easter Monday relief for Edinburgh Waverley. This was one of seven such trains that day, four of which departed from the Low Level platforms and ran via Airdrie and Bathgate.

4-4-0 No.2401 DANDIE DINMONT and banked by V2 2-6-2 No.953. The train took over sixteen minutes to reach Cowlairs, both locomotives slipping violently and almost continuously in the smoke-filled tunnel and cuttings. In contrast, excellent runs were made by D34 4-4-0 No.2484 GLEN LYON on 9th March and sister locomotive No.2493 GLEN GLOY on 30th March, albeit with pilot assistance on the bank. My best run was on 20th April with A3 No.37 HYPERION, admittedly in much improved weather conditions and with a load of no more than six corridors and two non-corridors. Banked by N15 0-6-2T No.9127, the train passed Cowlairs in just 5½ minutes.

On 1st June 1957, J37 0-6-0 No.64639 makes a brisk departure from Queen Street platform 8 with the 12.36pm for Kirkintilloch. It was followed by B1 No.61354 on the 12.43pm relief to York and A1 Pacific No.60160 AULD REEKIE on the 1.00pm for Edinburgh Waverley. At the time, the Kirkintilloch service comprised seven trains from Queen Street main line station, plus one originating at Hyndland from the Low Level platforms. With no trains on Saturday afternoons nor, needless to say, on Sundays, it was of limited appeal to potential travellers and withdrawal in 1964 came as no surprise.

With a banker at the rear, Standard 5MT 4-6-0 No.73108 blasts up Cowlairs Incline on 20th July 1957 with the 9.20am 'Evening Citizen TV Show Train' from Glasgow Queen Street to St. Andrews. The train of ex-LNER coaches had closed circuit television, installed at Cowlairs Works, as well as a studio and buffet facilities, and was a pioneering concept by the Scottish Region. Its first outing was to Oban in 1956 and in addition to public excursions, the train was available for school trips and private hire. The last run took place during 1962.

On 1st June, my last run before going overseas, a valiant effort was made by D11 No.2684 WIZARD OF THE MOOR, piloted by N15 No.9183 and banked by No.9131. The train was heavily loaded with eleven coaches but took only six minutes to Cowlairs, resulting in a near punctual arrival at Waverley. Also of note was the performance the previous week of D11 No.2674 FLORA MACIVOR with ten coaches and N15 No.9183 banking. Having taken eight minutes to pass Cowlairs, the engine ran so briskly that, despite thick mist, an on-time arrival was achieved at Waverley. On 13th April, when the 9.10pm was worked by V2 No.958, the banker was of interest, being No.9120

In a scene reminiscent of the days when the Caledonian was grudgingly allowed to use North British metals for access to Stobcross, 'Jumbo' 0-6-0 No.57446 passes Cowlairs East Junction with a goods train from the Springburn line to Cadder Yard on the main Edinburgh & Glasgow route. The date is 16th August 1958. On the right, Black 5 No.44967 heading a train of empty stock waits for the road on the spur from Cowlairs North Junction. The relatively new repair shop at Eastfield shed forms the backdrop.

of class N14. This small batch of six locos pre-dated the N15s, from which they differed in having a shorter cab.

One last memory of Queen Street during the final year of the LNER. On Sunday 18th May I returned from embarkation leave by the 9.30am King's Cross train, made up of six new Thompson coaches, a triple-articulated restaurant car, an accompanying 1st class coach and a bogie brake, standing at platform 2. The remainder of the train, three Gresley coaches reserved for the Carl Rosa Opera Company, was at platform 1 headed by V2 No.951 piloted by apple green B1 4-6-0 No.1117. With these added to the main part of the train, the two engines were out of sight in the tunnel, so that when the 'right away' was given the banker, N15 No.9183 only managed to compress the train's buffers. A porter then ran up the platform blowing a whistle, but still the footplate crew were oblivious. Finally a member of the station staff was dispatched into the tunnel to alert them and the fourteen coach cavalcade got on the move. Eight minutes were taken to Cowlairs, where the B1 was detached. With the train diverted via Falkirk Grahamston because of engineering work, Waverley was not reached until 11.19am. British Railways numbers of the above locos can be gained by adding 60000.

TOP OF THE BANK

Cowlairs, at the top of the incline out of Queen Street High Level Station, formed a focal point of interest. There was the locomotive works, Cowlairs station and the carriage sidings at West Junction where the Maryhill line went off. At East Junction, adjacent to Eastfield running shed, the line from Queen Street Low Level via Bellgrove and Springburn joined the Edinburgh & Glasgow route and there was a spur to North Junction.

Glasgow Fair Saturday, 16th July 1960, got off to a sunny start. I arrived at Cowlairs East Junction as A3 Pacific No.60057 ORMONDE came off the incline with the 10.40am special from Queen Street to Scarborough, composed of LMS corridors. When the N15 banker dropped off at West Junction, the train was running five minutes late. Then, B1 4-6-0 No.61081 emerged from the Springburn line with the six coach 10.30am special from Queen Street Low Level to Arbroath. The 8.40am from Leven – B1 No.61358 with eight non-corridors instead of the usual diesel multiple unit – went down to the High Level station some twenty minutes late. This was followed at 11.05am by K3 2-6-0 No.61916, shedded at Carlisle Canal, with an unidentified seven coach train. The 10.51 special for Scarborough came up from the terminus hauled by

A1 Pacific No.60161 NORTH BRITISH and the 'Queen of Scots' Pullman at 11.00am had Standard 5MT 4-6-0 No.73104 in charge. The 10.00am from Edinburgh Waverley consisted of a pair of Cross-Country diesel sets, then came B1 No.61181 with a relief and V2 2-6-2 No.60836 on a parcels train, this loco then working the 3.50pm to Saltburn. The 11.10am from Queen Street to St. Andrews passed at 11.30am and was hauled by B1 No.61133, replacing a diesel multiple unit, while the 11.16am relief for Elie had Ivatt mogul No.43137 on seven corridors.

The 11.30am Intercity dmu arrival from Edinburgh Waverley was ten minutes late, but timekeeping generally was reasonable for a busy summer Saturday. B1 No.61102 with eight corridors formed the 11.45am special to Whitley Bay and No.61197 was on the 11.45am from Low Level to Elie. Meanwhile, the 11.40am to Thornton Junction, normally a dmu, was hauled by B1 No.61404. The roster board at Eastfield shed showed an interesting working still to come, namely Clan Pacific No.72007 CLAN MAC-KINTOSH on the 12.12pm special from Helensburgh to Edinburgh. But, overall, traffic was somewhat down on previous years, as was the variety of motive power.

One of the most important feeders to the Edinburgh & Glasgow main line into Queen Street was the route from Helensburgh and Dumbarton. Snowplough-fitted Black 5 No.44957 of Eastfield shed passes Maryhill Park station with a freight from the West Highland line on 28th March 1956. The spur from Knightswood South Junction comes in on the left.

Chapter 3
SOUTH SIDE

Despite its great extent, varied nature and complex railway network, the area south of the Clyde from Paisley to Rutherglen is best dealt with as an entity as far as these reminiscences are concerned. Across Glasgow Bridge from the city centre, the infamous tenements of Gorbals and Hutchesontown dominated the routes out of Glasgow to the south. Beyond them, better housing formed districts such as Pollokshields and Govanhill, while further out, Giffnock and Netherlee were quite affluent. To the west, docks, shipbuilding and heavy engineering flanked the Clyde through Govan and Renfrew, with housing schemes such as Mosspark and Pollok occupying former farmland away from the river. To the east, the ancient Burgh of Rutherglen became absorbed by the spreading city, while remaining independent.

Three significant railways converged on Glasgow from the south. The Glasgow & Paisley Joint line from Paisley to Bridge Street opened in 1840 and was an immediate success, being fed at Paisley by busy routes from Ayr (1839-40) and Greenock (1841). Having absorbed the local companies which built these lines, the Glasgow & South Western and Caledonian worked the Joint line between them from 1850.

Another local railway opened from Barrhead to a terminus at South Side during 1848. This also became G&SW/Caledonian Joint in 1873, just before the link from Carlisle and Kilmarnock to Barrhead was completed. Finally, the Clydesdale Junction Railway to South Side opened in 1849. Eventually it became part of the Caledonian trunk route from Carlisle via Beattock. These three southern approaches to Glasgow really came into their own when bridges were built over the Clyde and the terminus stations at St Enoch and Central opened in 1876 and 1879 respectively. A whole series of local lines were also built, creating an intricate system which largely remains open for suburban traffic today. Notable were the Paisley Canal route (1885), the celebrated Cathcart Circle (1886-94) and the Lanarkshire & Ayrshire tracks through Neilston, Cathcart and Kirkhill (1903-04).

SOJOURNS AT CENTRAL
During the early 1950s, while working in Glasgow (although residing outside the city), I would often look in at one or other of the main line termini during my lunch break. Central station was a favourite as in the space of half an hour there was an exceptional amount of interest. The 1.24pm arrival from Edinburgh Princes Street would frequently bring in a Polmadie Pacific (or sometimes a 2-6-4T!), its three non-corridors then forming the 1.37pm to Kirkhill worked by a Balornock Compound or a loco running in from St Rollox Works. 'The Midday Scot', departing at 1.30pm, had a Coronation or, less frequently, a Princess Royal Pacific in charge. Both the 1.45pm to Liverpool and Manchester and the 1.53pm local for Carlisle were hauled by Jubilees. However, on one occasion, the 1.45pm was headed by a rebuilt Scot, No 46104 SCOTTISH BORDERER, while an unrebuilt member of the class, No 46151 THE ROYAL HORSE GUARDSMAN, stood alongside with 'The Midday Scot'.

On the dreich winter morning of 23rd January 1960, Coronation Pacific No.46247 CITY OF LIVERPOOL departs from platform 2 at Glasgow Central with the 10.00am 'Royal Scot' for London Euston. Part of the mighty roof dating from the rebuilding of 1901-1906 can be seen on the left. Appropriately, No.46235 CITY OF BIRMINGHAM was on the 10.05am for its namesake city. Sadly, the use of steam traction on principal West Coast services was drawing to a close by this time.

On Good Friday, 15th April 1960, Patriot 4-6-0 No.45517 has arrived at platform 1 of Central station with the morning service from Liverpool and Manchester. Long distance trains were running up to two hours late that day because of what was described as 'permanent way work and modernisation south of Crewe'. In marked contrast to steam traction, a poster above the tender boasts that 'Britain Leads in Nuclear Power'.

Interest could be augmented by liner specials from Greenock Princes Pier, as on 9th November 1950, when 2-6-4T No.42197 arrived with Trans-Atlantic passengers from Canadian Pacific's 'Empress of Scotland'. There were also the midweek football specials, as on 29th November 1950, when a Scotland v England game at Ibrox resulted in six departures between 1.00pm and 2.00pm, each composed of eight non-corridors, hauled by Black Five No.45475, Fairburn 2-6-4Ts Nos.42168, 42246 and 42692, ex-Caledonian 0-4-4T No.55268 and 'Jumbo' 0-6-0 No.57433. Adding to the variety that day were Aviemore's Caley bogie No.54466, ex-works on the 1.37pm to Kirkhill and Compound No.41139 on the 1.53pm 'Parly' to Carlisle. A sobering reminder of war occurred on 1st December 1950, when olive green hospital coach WD 207 was attached empty to 'The Midday Scot', having arrived on an overnight Euston train with Scots soldiers wounded in Korea.

Traffic during the build up to Christmas 1950 was exceptionally heavy and on 23rd December a points failure at Euston combined with a loco failure on the West Coast main line resulted in overnight trains not arriving in Glasgow until early afternoon! The

Immaculate Polmadie Coronation Pacific No.46220 CORONATION, complete with a crown on the smokebox door, made a stirring sight as it passed Eglinton Street station with the 10.00am up 'Royal Scot' on Coronation Day 1953. The backdrop of sandstone tenements would soon be exchanged for the sweeping moors of Beattock where the train no doubt looked even more impressive. Photograph K.K. MacKay.

A very typical South Side suburban scene, stretching back through the LMS era to Caledonian Railway days. McIntosh 0-4-4T No.55189, built at St Rollox Works, but subsequently disfigured by a stovepipe chimney, passes through Eglinton Street station on 8th September 1955 with the 5.39pm Cathcart Inner Circle train from Glasgow Central. The engine, restored to Caley condition as No.419, now works on the SRPS Bo'ness & Kinneil Railway, but Eglinton Street station closed in 1965.

model railway encircling Central station's Christmas tree that year had a Bassett Lowke 'O' gauge DUCHESS OF MONTROSE in the short-lived blue livery, with three 'blood and custard' coaches. Queen Street's tree had Hornby 4-4-2 FLYING SCOTSMAN. At the time, both pre-war and post-war LMS liveries were still to be seen at Central, together with the BR version of Caley

blue, Great Western green and LNWR black. On 20th December, rebuilt Patriot No.45531 SIR FREDERICK HARRISON, in experimental light green with red, cream and grey lining, worked the 1.45pm to Liverpool and Manchester. On 23rd February 1951, A1 Pacific No.60152 (not yet named HOLYROOD and still in LNER apple green) was observed on the 11.37am

from Edinburgh Princes Street. An evening visit to Central station on Fair Friday, 13th July 1951, found a lengthy queue for the Isle of Man via Ardrossan, with 'Crab' 2-6-0 No.42749 on ten non-corridors loading up at platform 13. Specials for Euston, with sleeping cars and reserved seating, made up to fourteen vehicles and hauled by rebuilt Scots, left at 7.55pm (No.46121

Fairburn 2-6-4T No.42060 passes Muirhouse Junction, bound for Terminus Junction and the Paisley Joint line at Shields Junction with an evening excursion from East Kilbride to Gourock on 2nd June 1956. The line from Central station comes in centre left and Pollokshields East station on the adjacent Cathcart Circle, scene of a macabre shooting in 1945, is overshadowed by Coplawhill tram works.

HIGHLAND LIGHT INFANTRY, CITY OF GLASGOW REGIMENT), 8.10pm (No.46128 THE LOVAT SCOUTS) and 8.35pm (No.46118 ROYAL WELCH FUSILIER with LNER stock including two restaurant cars). Another at 8.45pm had Coronation No.46221 QUEEN ELIZABETH in charge.

Wednesday 16th January 1952 was a day of particular interest, for when the Edinburgh Princes Street train arrived at platform 5, on time at 1.24pm despite several inches of snow, it was hauled by new Class 6 Pacific No.72000 CLAN BUCHANAN, which had been named the previous day by Glasgow's Lord Provost. The engine looked extremely smart in its dark green livery, with scarlet backing to its brass nameplates and was complete with a 66A shed plate and Caley route indicator. The press reported that it was one of a new class of ten being built at Crewe and described the loco as '130 tons of power and steel to be used on the Carlisle line'. On 28th January, No.72002 CLAN CAMPBELL, with nameplates covered, worked the 1.45pm to Liverpool and Manchester which left eleven minutes late in wintry weather to the sound of 'thunderous exhaust', according to my notes. The class were soon regular performers on this train. Although the Clans acquired a poor reputation, my friend Peter Brock, a former Kingmoor fireman with the benefit of practical experience with them, avers that they steamed well and were much superior to the Jubilees.

KILMACOLM COMMUTING

From 1950 to 1953 I commuted (to use the modern term) between Kilmacolm and Glasgow. My morning train was almost always the 8.41am (later 8.40am) which had left Greenock Princes Pier, unfortunately bereft of its Clyde Coast steamer services by then, at 8.20am for the punishing climb to Upper Port Glasgow, followed by a downhill sprint to Kilmacolm. It then called at Bridge of Weir and Houston & Crosslee before running non-stop from Paisley Canal to St Enoch, reached at 9.13am. Motive power for the five ex-LMS non-corridors was a Princes Pier 4-4-0, normally one of the Caley variety, of which the shed had nine or so during this period, although decrepit Compounds would occasionally appear from store at Ladyburn shed. Corkerhill 2Ps and even Kingmoor 'Crabs' were also seen, while towards the end of my stay Fairburn 2-6-4T No.42691, initially on loan from Polmadie, became a regular performer, with a marked improvement in timekeeping.

Unless having a night on the town (in which case I would get the 9.10pm, 10.25pm, or even the late train at 10.55pm on Saturdays – all of them Princes Pier turns) I would return by the 5.07pm from St Enoch. This ran via Paisley Canal, calling also at Crookston and Elderslie and was almost always powered by a Corkerhill 2-6-4T. On 4th January 1952, the 11.37am from Edinburgh Princes Street to Glasgow Central was worked by Standard 4MT

2-6-4T No.80023, the first of the class I had seen. Newly built at Brighton, it was running-in before going to the Great North of Scotland section. A week later, No.80024 appeared on the 5.07pm and thereafter the class monopolised the working of this train. On very rare occasions, I had to travel by the dreaded 5.36pm which called practically everywhere (except, incredibly, Paisley Canal) and took 48 minutes for the 18 miles! On Saturdays, my train was the 12.07pm which made intermediate stops at Shields Road, Paisley Gilmour Street and Bridge of Weir. It was allowed a leisurely 37 minutes to Kilmacolm and was usually worked by a Corkerhill Fairburn 2-6-4T or 2P 4-4-0, although Fowler 2-6-4T No.42420 from Ladyburn shed made an appearance, as did No.42380.

Looking back, perhaps the most exciting incident came on the morning of 25th September 1952 when a stranger in the shape of Fairburn 2-6-4T No.42057 ran in ahead of time (in itself an unusual event) and immediately had its fire dropped because of an injector failure, the sleepers being set ablaze as a result! A replacement locomotive was summoned from Princes Pier and in the shape of Caley bogie No.54506, arrived commendably quickly. This hauled the train back to the signal box, then ran round to shunt the tank into the goods yard. Crews were switched and we got away only some 35 minutes late. On a previous occasion, 2nd May 1951, the 8.40am suffered a delay of no less than

Fairburn 2-6-4T No.42128 approaches Pollokshaws East with the 5.30pm Cathcart Outer Circle train from Glasgow Central on 21st April 1960. Note the Caley route indicator on the bunker. The signal box was closed on 16th October 1961 in connection with the Cathcart re-signalling scheme.

Class 2P 4-4-0 No.40651 and Fairburn 2-6-4T No.42190 await departure from platform 1 of Glasgow St Enoch on 19th June 1954, with the ten coach 10.40am 'Empress Voyager' for Greenock Princes Pier, connecting with the Canadian Pacific liner 'Empress of Scotland' bound for Canada. Similar specials, under the name 'Cunarder', were run for Cunard sailings. The building above No.42190 and the leading vehicle housed the Goods Accounts Office, where I was employed for a short time. The work was unbelievably boring, but compensation was provided by a bird's eye view of movements at the station.

69 minutes when No.54508 stalled in the tunnels at Greenock. The train eventually arrived propelled by Fairburn No.42190 off the following 9.16am from the Pier. The 4-4-0 then reversed into the goods yard, where Jumbo No.57300 was shunting the daily pick-up, and the tank rounded to draw the train into the station, which was left at 9.49am.

One of the hazards of winter travel in those days was the frequency of fog which blanketed the Forth-Clyde valley, sometimes for days on end, accompanied by freezing temperatures. Thus, on 21st January 1952, in a covering of frozen snow and with the compartment windows thickly coated with ice (on the inside!), the 8.40am pulled out six minutes late behind 4-4-0 No.54479 to be almost immediately engulfed in what seemed like cotton wool. The first delay came at Bridge of Weir's outer home and we left here fourteen minutes late to crawl past Cart Junction. A signal stop at Elderslie was followed by another at Paisley West and then again at Paisley Canal. We left here 26 minutes late, only to be promptly brought to a stand again. Then came a crawl from signal to signal, to the muffled sound of exploding detonators, past Hawkhead, Crookston, Corkerhill, Bellahouston and Port Eglinton Junction boxes. Arrival at fog-bound St Enoch was 43 minutes late at 9.56am.

With darkness, conditions worsened and the 4.36pm arrival from Princes Pier (the stock of which formed the 5.07pm) came into its usual platform 5

some twenty minutes late. After another twenty minutes, No.80025 emerged from the pea souper hanging over the river and we got away at 5.23pm. Surprisingly, there was a more or less clear run (fogmen had been on duty all day) to Corkerhill No.1 box. Having passed the loco shed, where braziers stood at the coaling plant and under the water columns and dead engines were ringed by little fires to prevent them freezing up, we were stopped at No.2 box. Owing to a reduction in gas pressure, the cabin was in darkness, so the signalman worked as best he could by the light of a handlamp. Platforms at Corkerhill and Crookston were unlit for the same reason. Paisley Canal was left 27 minutes late, we were stopped at Ferguslie box, and brought to a near stand before drawing into Elderslie station. As we pulled out, 2-6-4T No.42210 came up alongside us with the 5.15pm for Ayr, to the alarm of some passengers. But all was well, for we diverged down the burrowing single track link to Cart Junction. By Bridge of Weir, visibility was down to ten yards and we groped our way to Kilmacolm, arriving 37 minutes late at 6.25pm. However, fog had already caused a serious accident on the Central Low Level line earlier in the day. The 6.50am from Rutherglen to Dalmuir, crowded with shipyard workers, ran into the back of the 6.40am to Old Kilpatrick, which was taking water at Clydebank station. The coaches telescoped and twenty passengers were injured.

As a postscript to these early commuting days, it is worth noting that Kilmacolm, with its red sandstone building, glass canopy and hanging flower baskets, won best-kept station awards, thanks to the eagle eye of stationmaster Dick Smith (no relation). Today, it is a restaurant after a period of dereliction following the withdrawal of the diesel multiple unit service for which it had become the terminus.

IF YOU CAN'T BEAT THEM...

By 1954 we were back in Glasgow, and for the next ten years occupied a house on the fringe of Pollokshields. This backed on to the Paisley Canal line opposite Bellahouston No.1 signal box, which controlled the entrance to Bellahouston carriage sidings. Shields Junction, on the Paisley Joint line stood in the background. There was also a view of the Clydesdale Junction line, so that, all in all, there was considerable scope for note taking!

Commuting, however, was a piecemeal affair with several alternatives available, none particularly convenient. Closest to hand was tram service 3 (replaced by buses in 1959) while probably more reliable, but furthest away, was the Corporation Underground at Shields Road. By train, there were stations at Bellahouston & Dumbreck on the Canal line, Maxwell Park on the Cathcart Circle and six-platform Shields Road which served both Central and St Enoch.

In leisurely fashion, Leeds Holbeck Jubilee No.45568 WESTERN AUSTRALIA passes Shields Road station with the 7.10pm relief 'Starlight Special' from Glasgow St Enoch to London St Pancras, routed via Dalry and Kilmarnock, on 17th June 1955. These are the Paisley Canal line platforms at Shields Road.

Initially, I used Bellahouston & Dumbreck station, once busy with the Bridgeton Cross 'bus trains', but now in a state of decline. There was a derelict brick building on the Gower Street overbridge (a replacement for the original wooden structure which had burnt down) with tickets obtained from an office on the Glasgow platform, adjacent to the carriage sheds. The former island platform carried the tall No.3 box of obvious Glasgow & South Western ancestry. The service matched the state of the run-down station, with a pencilled list of trains showing six to town (seven on Saturdays) and five in the opposite direction (four on Saturdays). In the morning I used the 9.02am (8.36am from Johnstone High) calling at Shields Road and taking eight minutes to St Enoch. Return was usually by the 5.36pm Princes Pier train which called additionally at Cumberland Street and was a 2-6-4T turn, very often No.42123. If going home for lunch I used the 1.00pm Paisley West train, hauled by an 0-4-4T and on Saturdays the 12.07pm to Shields Road.

The 9.02am, a seven coach set which went out empty to Johnstone, was usually worked by a Corkerhill 2P 4-4-0. During the period I travelled, I noted some thirty examples of this class, including some from Ardrossan and Hurlford sheds. However, Black 5s, Standard and Fairburn 2-6-4Ts and

Caley 0-6-0s also appeared. Veteran 'Jumbo' No.57241 worked for several days during the spring of 1954, after which, Jubilee No.45693 AGAMEMNON made a one-off appearance running tender first. Early summer brought a dozen different Compounds, from winter storage as well as locos drafted in from elsewhere for additional seasonal traffic worked by Corkerhill shed.

Despite the mixed motive power and much tender-first running, timekeeping was very reasonable and there were few out of course incidents. Nevertheless, on 25th January 1954, No.40594 sped through non-stop. With commendable alacrity, the signalman stopped the following 8.20am from Princes Pier (to the indignation of the crew of No.42691) for the three fare-paying passengers and two railwaymen. Three weeks later the train failed to appear, having broken down at Corkerhill, whilst on 22nd February No.40599 was replaced at Bellahouston No.1 box by sister engine No.40620. On 1st March, a large part of Glasgow was without electricity owing to an accident at Dalmarnock power station, St Enoch station being devoid of both lighting and trains because of the failure of the emergency supply. Power was partially restored later in the day at St Enoch, thanks to a diesel generator courtesy of the Army. On 14th April, the 5.36pm, unusually with a 2P

4-4-0, left 25 minutes late following confusion caused by the derailment of Caley bogie No.54508 at Gorbals Junction. The engine had fallen against the parapet of the bridge over Clelland Street. Fortunately this held, although coal from the tender covered the road below!

Upon descending from the 5.36pm at Bellahouston on 24th August I found that the threatened closure of the station was about to materialise. A chalked notice read '20th September 1954. On and after the above date passenger services from this station will be withdrawn.' On the last day, Saturday 18th September, the 9.02am was worked by Fowler 4F 0-6-0 No.43996 and the last train, the 5.46pm from St Enoch to Paisley West, on which I travelled, had 0-4-4T No.55211 in charge. Thereafter, I used Shields Road station, which had some thirty trains to Glasgow Central and about forty to St Enoch. Soon, I was to follow the adage 'if you can't beat them, join them' by becoming an employee of the Scottish Region of British Railways. However, that is another story. Today, Bellahouston is once again served by rail. With the reopening of the Canal line in 1990, a new station was provided at Dumbreck, a short distance west of the old, and it has an undreamed-of half hourly service to Glasgow Central.

Ex-Caledonian 0-4-4T No.55206 leaves Bellahouston carriage sidings with empty stock for St Enoch on 31st May 1958. The view was taken from the kitchen window of my home in the Pollokshields district, giving a panoramic view across the Canal line and Paisley Joint line to Kinning Park goods depot. Tenements in Maclellan Street form the backdrop.

On the cloudy evening of 13th June 1956, Royal Scot No.46109 ROYAL ENGINEER lifts the 9.05pm sleeping car train from Glasgow St Enoch to London St Pancras through Neilston Low station on the 1 in 70 climb to Shilford summit on the Glasgow, Barrhead & Kilmarnock Joint line.

The 5.26pm from Bridgeton Central to Milngavie pauses at Partick Hill on the sunny evening of 30th May 1957 with J37 No.64573 in charge. Some of these sturdy ex-North British S class 0-6-0s were noted hauling trains of Sherman tanks from the docks during the War. Bridgeton Central was known as Bridgeton Cross during LNER days.

On the typically wet Fair Friday afternoon of 12th July 1957, Eastfield B1s Nos.61340 and 61344 roll into Partick Hill station with the 2.30pm special from Dumbarton Central to Newcastle, consisting of ten corridors and routed via Springburn. Numerous specials were required when Glasgow Fair was celebrated with relish at the end of the War.

CHAPTER 4

WEST SIDE NORTH BRITISH

When the Edinburgh & Glasgow Railway opened in 1842, the tract of country stretching westwards towards Old Kilpatrick, Bearsden and Milngavie at the foot of the Kilpatrick Hills was largely rural. There were pockets of industry on the north bank of the Clyde, but places such as Maryhill and Partick were mere villages. The sparkling River Kelvin in its steep sided valley could well have been a sylvan stream in a remote part of the Borders, although the Forth & Clyde Canal provided a touch of commercial activity. With the relentless expansion of docks, warehouses, shipyards and factories all the way from Stobcross to Old Kilpatrick during the second half of the nineteenth century, the character of the area changed completely. Away from the Clyde, thousands of tenements replaced farmland while hamlets gave their names to whole districts of the city. An intense suburban railway network eventually developed as well.

The Glasgow, Dumbarton & Helensburgh Railway opened in 1858. It ran from Cowlairs, at the top of the incline out of Queen Street, to Maryhill, Kilbowie, Dalmuir, Old Kilpatrick, Bowling, Dumbarton, and Helensburgh on the Firth of Clyde. Initially it was single track and very much a rural line. In 1863 a branch to Bearsden and

Milngavie was completed. With the construction of Queen's Dock, a line was built from Maryhill to Stobcross via Anniesland and Partick. It opened in 1874, together with the branch from Jordanhill to Whiteinch. Shipbuilding inspired the Glasgow, Yoker & Clydebank Railway, which opened from Jordanhill to Clydebank during 1882. Trains began running on the Glasgow, City & District line through Queen Street Low Level to Charing Cross, Finnieston and Stobcross in 1886. At the same time, a short branch opened to Hyndland in the fashionable West End. Finally, a vital link from Clydebank to Dalmuir on the Helensburgh line was completed in 1896. Although largely built by independent companies in a piecemeal manner, this complex network of lines was welded into a cohesive suburban system by the North British Railway.

THE VIEW FROM THE WINDOW

Following the Clydeside blitz of 1941 (see *Glasgow's Trams - The Twilight Years*, published by Irwell Press in 1998) we moved from Hyndland to nearby Broomhill, which was a real bonus as far as I was concerned. From our flat there was an excellent view of the LNER Queen Street Low Level Line from Partick Junction, where the sharply-curved and steeply-graded Hyndland

branch diverged, to Whiteinch loop sidings near the triangular junction where the routes through Anniesland and Jordanhill parted company. Although the line was several hundred yards away there was an uninterrupted view across wartime allotments, long since given over to housing. From a side window there was a glimpse of the LMS Central Low Level Line near Crow Road station.

Initially, it must be admitted, I thought of both lines as suburban backwaters, but soon came to realise that they were by no means devoid of interest – thus began my life-long habit of note taking. Although the LNER trains were mainly worked by V1 2-6-2Ts, supplemented by former North British 0-6-0s, with N2 0-6-2Ts and C16

Preserved North British Railway 4-4-0 No.256 GLEN DOUGLAS (BR class D34 No.62469) awaits departure from Hyndland terminus with the Stephenson Locomotive Society 'Glasgow City & District' railtour of 30th April 1960. The special ran via Springburn and the Monkland & Kirkintilloch line to Coatbridge, then took in Bothwell, Torrance and Dalmuir Park. These 'Glens' together with the 'Scotts' were once a familiar sight at Hyndland on the semi-fast trains from Leith Central and Edinburgh Waverley via Bathgate, Airdrie and Queen Street Low Level.

With Gartnavel Mental Hospital forming the backdrop in this 1st April 1961 view, Standard 4MT 2-6-0 No.76090, hauling empty stock forming the 11.53am to Airdrie, arrives at the new Hyndland station which materialised when the suburban lines were electrified. The timber extensions to the platforms were necessary to accommodate rakes of non-corridor steam-hauled coaches during temporary withdrawal of the 'Blue Trains' following serious electrical faults. Whiteinch loop sidings, the site of so much wartime activity, are on the right.

4-4-2Ts for shorter journeys, there were half a dozen Edinburgh-Hyndland trains which used the secondary route through Bathgate and Airdrie. These produced D11 4-4-0s, together with ex-North British Scotts, Glens and Intermediates. New B1 4-6-0s from the North British Locomotive Co. at Springburn also appeared in early post-war years. Another train worth watching was the 4.37pm from Springburn to Singer, nominally worked by an Eastfield K2 2-6-0 but quite often used as a

running-in turn for engines fresh out of Cowlairs Works. The engine returned on a workers' service from the huge sewing machine factory, usually composed of archaic stock, including six-wheelers.

Before the War, variety would have come from excursion trains, Sunday School trips and football specials, but these had been banned 'for the duration'. However, wartime traffic included double-headed troop trains (more frequent on the LMS line, actually) a hospital coach attached to certain

Helensburgh workings, naval gun barrels for the Clyde shipyards and whole trains of Sherman tanks hauled by J37s and banked by N15s. The sidings adjoining Whiteinch loop (at the site of the present Hyndland station) were used for staging traffic bound for Stobcross Yard, and new khaki-coloured austerity 2-8-0s built by the North British Locomotive Co. were daily visitors. Unfortunately, their tenders had a tendency to derail during shunting operations and the Eastfield breakdown

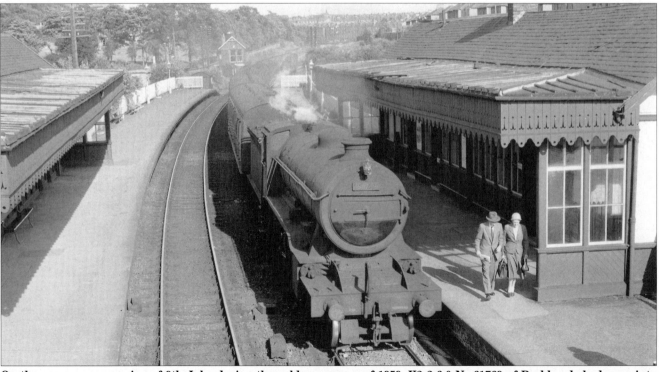

On the very sunny evening of 9th July, during the golden summer of 1959, K2 2-6-0 No.61769 of Parkhead shed runs into Jordanhill station with the 5.34pm from Bridgeton Central to Helensburgh. Visible in the background is Whiteinch Park East Junction signal box, where the Anniesland line came in from the left.

Class V3 2-6-2T No.67628 gets into its stride as it leaves Anniesland station with the 5.57pm from Bridgeton Central to Helensburgh on 2nd July 1958. The Maryhill spur passes behind Knightswood South Junction cabin on the left, whilst the start of the Knightswood goods branch is on the right. The V tanks were characteristic of the ex-North British suburban lines in the Glasgow area, from the 1930s to the advent of 'Blue Trains'.

crane was frequently called out. The Hyndland branch could also be a source of entertainment. Were a 4-4-0 to be stopped at the outer home signal in wet weather, there was a strong possibility of it being unable to restart the train, resulting in considerable delay while a loco was sent down from the terminus to assist.

The evening of 22nd April 1943 brought the totally unexpected sight of an N15 0-6-2T hauling a pair of US Army Transportation Corps 0-6-0Ts which had been unloaded at Stobcross Quay and were on their way to Cowlairs Works to be prepared for service. By the end of the year I had seen twenty such tanks, together with twenty of the 2-8-0s, although No.2315 was one of the very few seen at work, on 23rd June. On 13th June V2 2-6-2 No.3688 was a

On the frosty morning of 2nd January 1958, V3 2-6-2T No.67628 arrives at Westerton with the 11.48am from Milngavie to Bridgeton Central. Normally this train ran to Springburn, but that station was one of those closed for the New Year holiday.

Standard Class 4 Mogul No.76103 leaves Milngavie with the 5.25pm to Westerton on 28th August 1961. Meanwhile Stanier 2-6-4T No.42426 takes water in the goods yard prior to working the 6.06pm to Airdrie. This was one of the locos drafted in when steam made an unexpected comeback upon temporary withdrawal of the 'Blue Trains'.

unique visitor with a freight, the engine having been newly built at Darlington. During that summer, the stock of supposedly barred holiday traffic reliefs was seen coming from Queen Street Low Level, motive power including D49 4-4-0 No.2753 CHESHIRE, B12 4-6-0 No.8543, V4 2-6-2 No.3401 BANTAM COCK, and K3 2-6-0 No.3823. A fifteen coach train was double headed by a J39 0-6-0 and a V1 2-6-2T, while C16 4-4-2T No.9513 piloted D11 4-4-0 No.6389 HAYSTOUN OF BUCKLAW on a twelve coach formation. On Glasgow Fair Saturday, B12 4-6-0 No.8504 stood by in Whiteinch loop with a train of corridor stock for Edinburgh or the Fife Coast, as required. No such workings took place the following year.

Arriving home from school one afternoon in early January 1944, I noticed what seemed to be a WD 2-8-0 on shunting duty. On closer inspection it proved to be WD 2-10-0 No.3653, and these soon became as familiar a sight as the eight-coupled locos. At the end of that month a pair of 2-8-0+0-8-2 narrow gauge Garratts in dismantled state were seen on flat wagons bound for the docks and shipment overseas. Despite the war being at a critical stage in the lead up to the D-Day Landings, and the railway system with little spare capacity, the usual summer Sunday service of eight trains each way operated between Bridgeton Cross and Helensburgh. With 'Holidays at Home' the order of the day, these trains could be extremely heavily loaded, so much so that in fine weather the last two departures from the coast, at 8.20pm and 9.30pm, would be made

up of twelve non-corridors which, full and standing, was no mean feat for a V1 tank. Some Saturday interest was provided by the 6.45pm from Thornton Junction which used Queen Street Low Level. The stock continued to Cowlairs via Maryhill, 'Directors' and 'Glens' being the motive power.

During the early evening of 23rd January 1945, two light engines coming down Cowlairs Incline collided with a train of empty stock in the tunnel, effectively closing Queen Street station for some twelve hours. Main line traffic was diverted through the Low Level platforms and I became aware of this when J37 0-6-0 No.9123 passed with

ten empty corridors to form an Edinburgh service. This and subsequent workings were routed via Springburn, with locomotives changed at Eastfield shed because Pacifics and V2s were unable to use the Low Level, through clearance problems in the tunnels. Diverted trains continued to pass until the early hours, causing considerable delays to the local service. Another accident occurred on 1st May when the 12.29pm from Helensburgh to Bridgeton Cross came to grief at Partick Junction, with V1 2-6-2T No.2922 and the leading coach derailed. The tank was hauled back on to the track by a hawser attached to J38 0-6-0 No.1407.

Class	First LNER No.	1946 No.
V2 2-6-2	3683	971
D49 4-4-0	2753	2728 CHESHIRE
B12 4-6-0	8543	1543
V4 2-6-2	3401	1700 BANTAM COCK
K3 2-6-0	3823	1983
D11 4-4-0	6389	2682 HAYSTOUN OF BUCKLAW
C16 4-4-2T	9513	7499
B12 4-6-0	8504	1504
J37 0-6-0	9123	4558
V1 2-6-2T	2922	7622
J38 0-6-0	1407	5906
J38 0-6-0	1416	5914
J36 0-6-0	9755	5313
D30 4-4-0	9428	2437 ADAM WOODCOCK
J37 0-6-0	9303	4609
J37 0-6-0	9161	4563
D11 4-4-0	6388	2681 CAPTAIN CRAIGENGELT
D34 4-4-0	9406	2474 GLEN CROE
D49 4-4-0	265	2705 LANARKSHIRE
D34 4-4-0	9149	2467 GLENFINNAN
D30 4-4-0	9500	2441 BLACK DUNCAN

Relatively new Drumry station, situated between Drumchapel and Singer and built to serve a Corporation housing estate, looking west on 16th May 1956.

On VE Day, 8th May 1945, J38 0-6-0 No.1416 was unusual motive power for a Helensburgh train. Even stranger was the use of J36 0-6-0 No.9755 on 30th May and D30 4-4-0 No.9428 ADAM WOODCOCK on 1st June. Glasgow Fair Saturday, 14th July, started at 8.15am when J37 0-6-0 No.9303 arrived at Whiteinch loop to pick up eight corridors bound for Queen Street Low Level, followed by No.9161, also with eight corridors. Meanwhile, D11 4-4-0 No.6388 CAPTAIN CRAIGENGELT and D34 4-4-0 No.9406 GLEN CROE had passed with ten on, and D49 4-4-0 No.265 LANARKSHIRE came from Queen Street Low Level with eleven empties. A further twenty or so specials were seen during the course of the day with several 'cops' for my Ian Allan ABC, notably D34 No.9149 GLENFINNAN and D30 No.9500 BLACK DUNCAN. A mixed bag of coaching stock included clerestory-roofed non-corridors, former green and cream tourist stock and Southern Railway vehicles. 'Pande-

monium' was how the Queen Street stationmaster described the day to a newspaper reporter, the most congested trains being those for Fife. 'They were packed like herrings in a box, but we've been digging up extras all day and we've got them off o.k.' Truly, World War Two was over!

These pre-1946 LNER locomotive numbers may not be familiar to many readers, so the later designation is shown in the table(opposite). The BR number can be identified by adding 60,000 to the 1946 number. For example, V2 No.971 becomes 60971. The order conforms with that in the text.

V3 2-6-2T No.67632 draws to a stand at Bowling station with the 8.00pm from Helensburgh Central to Bridgeton Central on 31st May 1958. This was the terminus of the Caledonian & Dumbartonshire Railway from Balloch, opened in 1850, until the Glasgow-Helensburgh line was completed eight years later.

On 22nd July 1959, a few days before the station closed, a solitary passenger stands on the platform at Anderston Cross awaiting the arrival of the 5.40pm from Maryhill Central to Whifflet Upper, hauled by Standard 4MT 2-6-0 No.76002. The columns had been denuded of their canopies. Anderston Cross re-opened twenty years later as part of the electrified Argyle Line, the suffix once beloved of Glasgow for road junctions being dropped.

With a brake van in tow, ex-Caledonian 'Jumbo' 0-6-0 No.57296 uses the facing crossover in Stobcross station to reach Stobcross Yard at Queen's Dock on 23rd July 1959. This engine was a long-term resident at Dawsholm shed. Solid columns supporting massive overhead girders, together with a gloomy tunnel mouth and strong retaining walls, encapsulate the atmosphere of Glasgow Central Railway stations, all the way from Botanic Gardens to Dalmarnock.

CHAPTER 5
WEST SIDE CALEDONIAN

For many years, the North British had a virtual monopoly of traffic to and from the ever-increasing concentration of docks and industrial establishments along the north bank of the Clyde. Despite having been granted running powers to Queen's Dock in 1874, the Caledonian was very frustrated by this situation. The remedy came late in the century and was a spectacular one, involving two nominally independent lines which were very expensive to build. Indeed, one of them tunnelled through the very heart of the city and ventured into some of the more sedate parts of the West End, where it had to be hidden from view. In addition to capturing a large share of the abundant commercial traffic on offer, the Caley helped meet the almost insatiable demand for suburban passenger services.

The Glasgow Central Railway was authorised in 1888 and ran from the East End to Dawsholm and Maryhill via Central Low Level, Stobcross and Kelvin Bridge. A large proportion of it was underground, including the middle section beneath Argyle Street which required some extraordinary feats of engineering. The Lanarkshire & Dumbartonshire Railway was not sanctioned until 1891 because of interminable wrangling with the North British over the original plan to extend as far west as Balloch on Loch Lomond. In its final form the line ran from Stobcross to Dumbarton via Partick, Scotstoun, Clydebank and Dalmuir. There was also a branch from Partick to Possil which had junctions with the Glasgow Central Railway near Maryhill and met an existing branch from Rutherglen, thus creating a route for goods traffic round the north side of the city. Passenger services over most of this system commenced in 1896.

COMMUTING FROM CROW ROAD
For a few weeks in the late autumn of 1946, while awaiting call up for the army, I took temporary employment with a photographic processing firm in the east end of Glasgow and travelled daily by train from Crow Road station to Bridgeton Cross. The LMS weekly zone ticket cost 2s 7d (less than 13p!). My morning train was the 7.46am from Possil to Coatbridge Central which left Crow Road at 7.55am and was scheduled to arrive at Bridgeton Cross at 8.13am. It was a three coach set hauled almost exclusively by ex-Caledonian 0-4-4T No.15168 (built at St. Rollox 1900), the one exception during the period in question being

'Jumbo' 0-6-0 No.17428 (dating from 1897).

Homeward-bound, my train was nominally the 5.48pm Rutherglen to Dalmuir, leaving Bridgeton Cross at 5.54pm. This was unique, for in order to serve Crow Road it made a detour via Bellshaugh Junction rather than running direct between Stobcross and Partick West. The train omitted a stop at Kelvin Bridge ('for University') and passed through the closed stations at Botanic Gardens, Kirklee and Kelvinside. But the actual service caught at Bridgeton Cross often varied, according to the volume of work to be done. It could be as early as the 4.25pm from Newton (via Carmyle) to Possil which left Bridgeton Cross at 4.57pm hauled by an 0-4-4T. This was

This could well be part of a splendid model railway layout! In reality it is the view from Benalder Street in Partick on 19th July 1961, as Standard 2-6-4T No.80086 heads the 5.19pm from Rutherglen to Possil out of Stobcross tunnel and across the River Kelvin towards Kelvin Hall station (formerly Partick Central). This section of the Lanarkshire & Dumbartonshire Railway was almost as difficult to construct as the Glasgow Central Railway, being partially sub-surface. The flour mill, now owned by Rank Hovis, is still in operation and the derelict railway bridge survives as well.

Black Five No.45169 at Kelvin Hall station on 17th September 1959 with the 6.37pm special returning to Dumfries from the Scottish Industries Exhibition. The street-level Lanarkshire & Dumbartonshire building was suitably decorated for the occasion. Formerly Patrick Central, the station retained its new name until closure in 1964.

something of an express as it did not call at Glasgow Green, Anderston Cross and Stobcross.

However, more often than not, I would get the 5.25pm (4.53pm Glenboig to Possil) which was always worked by a Stanier 2-6-2T (usually No.186), an

attraction being its patronage by young female workers from local factories! It was a heavily loaded train, with commuters lining the platform at Central Low Level and a swarm of shipyard workers boarding at Partick West, by which time there was standing

room only. On Saturdays (yes, we worked on Saturday mornings in those days) I would get the 12.21pm for Possil, which started at Bridgeton Cross and arrived empty stock from Rutherglen. My first journey produced veteran 'Jumbo' 0-6-0 No.17472 fitted with a stovepipe

Stanier 2-6-2T No.40153 runs into Crow Road station on 5th November 1960 with the 12.30pm from Maryhill Central to Coatbridge Central, the last but one city-bound service to use the station before its replacement by the new facilities at Hyndland, seen in the background. These were served by electric trains to and from Queen Street Low Level, inaugurated some ninety minutes earlier by Sir Brian Robertson, Chairman of the British Transport Commission.

Fairburn 2-6-4T No.42058 pauses at Yoker Ferry with the 5.16pm from Dalmuir Riverside to Rutherglen on 25th September 1964. This familiar Lanarkshire & Dumbartonshire scene, comprising an island platform on an embankment and generous Caledonian buildings with a wide canopy overlooked by sandstone tenements and riverside industry, soon disappeared for ever.

chimney and tender cab, with No.17470 also appearing subsequently.

Even half a century ago, the Central Low Level system seemed like a relic from a past era. Its atmosphere was compounded of smoke, steam, fog, echoing passageways and dripping walls, rounded off by the reverberating exhaust of steam locomotives pounding through the soot-encrusted tunnels. But timekeeping was remarkably good, bearing in mind that modern aids such as A.W.S. and colour light signalling were non-existent, and my only late arrivals were of three or four minutes. The system closed in 1964 and twenty years later Doris and I were to reside for a time in a modern block of flats occupying the site of Crow Road station.

VINTAGE STEAM TO THE EXHIBITION

The two week programme of 'Excursions by Historic Locomotives' for the Scottish Industries Exhibition at Kelvin Hall commenced on Saturday 5th September 1959 with trains from Aberdeen and Carlisle to Glasgow Central. The Aberdeen train was making an unadvertised call at Stirling to take water, so I travelled there by the 10.00am Glasgow Buchanan Street-Inverness and joined the Special which rolled in two minutes early. Ex-Great North of Scotland 4-4-0 No.49 GORDON HIGHLANDER (formerly class D40 No.62277) piloted ex-Great Western 'City' 4-4-0 No.3440 CITY OF

TRURO on six LMS corridors, but with only about forty passengers. Departure was punctual at 11.53am under a heat-hazed blue sky, the steady run at 55/60 mph preceding arrival at platform 4 of Central four minutes late at 12.50pm. Ex-Caledonian 4-2-2 No.123 (formerly LMS No.14010) and ex-North British 4-4-0 No.256 GLEN DOUGLAS (formerly class D34 No.62469) had worked the Carlisle train via Kilmarnock and Barrhead.

On the afternoon of Monday 7th September, ex-Highland 'Jones Goods' 4-6-0 No.103 (formerly LMS No.17916) made its first passenger working since restoration on an excursion from Largs to Kelvin Hall, this station having been renamed from Partick Central. No.49 acted as pilot. Unfortunately, No.256 failed that morning with the Edinburgh Princes Street-Kelvin Hall train, and for the return working a somewhat grimy No.62496 GLEN LOY was substituted, with No.123 piloting. No.62496, an Eastfield engine, was standby at Dawsholm shed for the remainder of the programme.

The following day, GLEN DOUGLAS failed at Shotts with the Edinburgh Special and No.123 took the six coach train on to Rutherglen where, at Dalmarnock Junction, bunker-first 2-6-4T No.42217 was attached to assist through the tunnels to Kelvin Hall. No.256 was, however, able to take up its scheduled return working as pilot to No.103 on a Coalburn train. On

Wednesday 9th September, No.3440 ran hot while working from Aberdeen and was 20 minutes late arriving at Central station. On the next day, Nos.103 and 256 arrived at Kelvin Hall from Wishaw, while on Friday 11th September the Glen was again in action, working an afternoon train (originating at Girvan) from Ayr in company with No.49. Saturday 12th September saw CITY OF TRURO arriving at Central ten minutes late with the 9.05am from Montrose, being followed by a B1 on a special from Leuchars Junction.

A favourite ploy with enthusiasts in the evening was to use the diesel multiple unit service to Kelvin Hall and return with one or more of the specials for the five minute rumble through the tunnels to Central Low Level. Thus I enjoyed runs behind Nos.49 and 103, 123 and 62496, 123 and 49, 49 and 256 and 256 and 103. On Monday 14th September, I travelled from Renfrew Wharf to Kelvin Hall by the 2.00pm special, consisting of seven non-corridors, worked by 123 and 103. The stock was brought down by the locos running tender first, No.123 having the thistles etched on its buffers protected by sacking. The locos then took water before propelling the coaches into the dilapidated wooden platform. It was devoid of any building and this obscure riverside terminus was normally patronised only by workers from nearby industrial establishments. In brilliant sunshine, a punctual departure was

On the dreich evening of 4th April 1958, Stanier 2-6-2T No.40188 calls at Clydebank Riverside with the 4.26pm from Balloch to Rutherglen to pick up workers from John Brown's Shipyard, the sheds of which can be seen in the background. On the left, 2-6-2T No.40200 takes water at the terminal platforms, which by this time were used by only a single train.

made for Fulbar Street, then South Renfrew and Paisley Abercorn where a school party joined. After traversing the west side of the triangle at Rutherglen, the train was held by signals in smoke-filled Glasgow Cross station, with the rumble of trams passing overheard clearly audible. After a call at Central Low Level, arrival at Kelvin Hall was punctual at 2.49pm, the empty stock then continuing to Bellshaugh Junction at Dawsholm. For the return working,

No.256 was substituted, as programmed, for No.123.

On Wednesday 16th September, 256 and 3440 were used from Aberdeen. Two days later, after a spell of duty at the rolling stock exhibition in Central station, I rounded off an unforgettable fortnight by travelling from the Low Level station on the return Edinburgh excursion which, hauled by 123 and 49, left one minute late at 9.36pm with thirteen passengers, mostly

enthusiasts. There was a signal stop in Dalmarnock station, a check to walking pace at Rutherglen to put down the pilotman and a two minute stand at Mossend No.4 Junction. Holytown station was left eight minutes late at 10.12pm. Crossing the moonlit countryside, arrival at Shotts was five minutes late at 10.26pm. Then came the anticlimax of a diesel multiple unit journey back to Glasgow.

More Caledonian elegance is apparent at Kilbowie on 4th April 1958 as Fairburn 2-6-4T No.42056 arrives with the 4.28pm from Dalmuir Riverside to Rutherglen. On the right is part of the huge Singer Factory, now replaced by a shopping centre and industrial estate. Even more impressive architecture appeared on the Glasgow Central Railway, notably at Kirklee, Botanic Gardens, Anderston Cross and Glasgow Cross.

A gathering of railwaymen and enthusiasts at dilapidated Dalmuir Riverside station on 3rd October 1964 mark the closure of the Central Low Level system. Standard Mogul No.76074 heads the last train, the 12.05pm for Rutherglen. Although the Dalmarnock-Stobcross section of the Glasgow Central Railway subsequently re-opened, there was no hope for the Lanarkshire & Dumbartonshire tracks, which were paralleled by electrified former North British lines.

Class D30 4-4-0 No.62429 THE ABBOT of Thornton shed passed through the grim confines of High Street station on 14th July 1956 with the 3.12pm Fair Saturday special from Glasgow Queen Street Low Level to Leven in Fife. The train, composed of seven non-corridor coaches, took the Springburn line. This ex-North British veteran was withdrawn in August 1957.

CHAPTER 6
EAST SIDE

The East End of Glasgow was characterised by rather drab tenements and heavy industry. Eventually, Corporation housing schemes and other developments extended the built up area towards the established coalfield towns of Coatbridge and Uddingston. Physically, this stretch of country north of the Clyde is rather featureless, although the occasional sandstone outcrop gave rise to low hills such as those at Mount Vernon. The Garnkirk & Glasgow was the only railway in the area for many years, and this was peripheral. South of the river, the Clydesdale Junction line through Rutherglen opened in 1849, both of these routes becoming important elements in the Caledonian network. A Caley branch from Rutherglen to Coatbridge was completed in 1866, but again this was marginal. However, from 1870 to 1897 a series of lines penetrated the East End proper and provided comprehensive suburban passenger services in addition to their main role as arteries of commerce.

Immediately prior to its take-over by the North British, the Edinburgh & Glasgow Railway promoted a line from Glasgow to Coatbridge, a logical extension of the existing tracks from Edinburgh to Coatbridge via Bathgate. Passenger services between Waverley and Glasgow College began in 1871. The Glasgow, Bothwell, Hamilton & Coatbridge Railway left this route at Shettleston in order to serve the coalfield, passenger trains commencing in 1878. Although the Bellgrove-Springburn section of the complex and convoluted City of Glasgow Union (North British and Glasgow & South Western) opened in 1875, passenger traffic over this northern limb had a painfully slow induction, from 1881 to 1887. Meanwhile, the Glasgow City & District from the West End and Queen Street Low Level to College (later High Street) had opened in 1886. Finally, the Caley created a fairly intricate network on the East Side, in little more than a decade. The Rutherglen-Dalmarnock branch of 1861 was extended to Blochairn Junction on the Garnkirk line during 1886 and on to Possil in 1896, paralleling the City of Glasgow Union and North British round the eastern and northern outskirts of the city. Glasgow Central Railway tracks from the West End and Central Low Level to Bridgeton Cross, Darlmarnock, Carmyle and Newton were complete in 1895-97.

THE END OF AN INTERLOPER

Now almost forgotten, with much of its infrastructure lost because of redevelopment, the former Glasgow, Bothwell, Hamilton & Coatbridge Railway, more prosaically known as the Hamilton (LNER) branch in later years, ran from Shettleston Junction through Mount Vernon, Uddingston and Bothwell, with a branch to Whifflet. Its main purpose was to tap a Caledonian-dominated part of the Lanarkshire coalfield. This was more or less worked

On 16th July 1960, Class 4 Mogul No.76105 traverses the Haghill Junction-Parkhead North spur with the 9.45am Fair Holiday special from Clydebank Central to Whitley Bay, routed by way of Springburn and Bathgate. A J36 0-6-0, No.65246, with two wagons for the local coal merchants, had been put into the goods loop to allow passage of a diesel multiple unit special from Airdrie to St. Andrews.

Uddingston West station, looking towards Bothwell, on 2nd July 1955. A peaceful scene but one about to disappear for ever, as passenger services were withdrawn that evening. The last train was the 6.09pm from Hyndland, hauled by N2 0-6-2T No.69510. Today, very little trace remains of this North British penetration of Caledonian territory.

out by the end of World War II, but the line enjoyed a brief renaissance under BR, with excursions to the Clyde coast and a new station called Calderpark Halt. This served Glasgow Zoo and gave rise to a summer Sunday service between Milngavie and Hamilton. However, the revival proved short-lived

and on 15th September 1952 the branch was cut back to Bothwell, owing to undermining of Craighead viaduct by colliery workings. Not unexpectedly, the truncated passenger service did not last long, and although somewhat surprisingly resumed after the disastrous ASLEF strike of 1955, was

withdrawn for good a fortnight later. The last day, Saturday 2nd July, was warm and partially sunny as I dropped down from the 1.52pm ex-Clydebank East at Mount Vernon station. After it had pulled out behind Class N2 0-6-2T No.69564, I photographed another N2, No.69510, hauling the 2.38pm from

Class V1 2-6-2T No.67678 at Uddingston East with the 3.56pm from Clydebank East to Bothwell on 2nd July 1955, the last day of service. Opened in 1878, this was one of the original stations on the Glasgow, Bothwell, Hamilton & Coatbridge Railway. Its neighbour, Uddingston West, opened in 1888.

On 22nd July 1963, Fairburn 2-6-4T No.42131 hauling the empty stock of the 4.58pm Dalmuir Riverside-Rutherglen descends from Strathclyde Junction towards the start of the underground section at Dalmarnock. The London Road line is on the left and the Cathkin Braes form the skyline.

Stanier 2-6-2T No.40188 crosses one of the parallel bridges over the Clyde as it leaves Rutherglen with the 12.28pm to Balloch, on 11th March 1961. This bridge has since been removed and present day electric services use the earlier one a few yards upstream.

Bothwell to Hyndland. The wooden station building stood on this side, half gutted by fire since the time a porter had attempted to thaw a gas pipe (instead of a frozen water pipe) with a blowlamp! I then set off to walk the somewhat weed-grown double track, crossing the Rutherglen & Coatbridge line and passing Broomhouse signal box, which was switched out. The station here had closed in 1927 and, although the overgrown platforms remained and there was a little used siding into a brickworks, the main feature of note was Mount Vernon greyhound racing track.

A short distance further on, and I was photographing Calderpark Halt which had been opened by Mrs Cameron, wife of the Chief Regional Officer, precisely four years previously. Immediately beyond was the imposing Calderbraes viaduct, spanning both the North Calder Water and the Bellshill road. After recording No.69510 with the 3.29pm from Hyndland and No.69564 with the 4.08pm from Bothwell, I followed the line through a wooded stretch and past the site of Maryville station, which closed as long ago as 1908, then past colliery sidings and along an embankment to Uddingston West station in its almost rural setting. As

at Broomhouse, the box was switched out, and as at Mount Vernon the porter presented me with a handful of tickets. The West Coast main line was then crossed; a little further on was Uddingston East station, which had a stone building with shortened awning.

I bought a ticket here, the booking clerk complaining that he was fed up with letters requesting such, and joined the 3.56pm ex-Clydebank East which left at 4.54pm hauled by V1 2-6-2T No.67678. We crossed fields as No.69510 went the other way on the 4.55pm to Hyndland. The derelict Coatbridge line came in on the left, sidings serving Bothwell gas works lay on the right, then we curved through a cutting into Bothwell station four minutes late at 4.59pm. The sandstone building was on the down platform, a wooden shelter stood on the other, and there was a signal box at the far end. Beyond here were Bothwell Castle Nos.1 and 2 pits, which had been closed in 1949, together with several rusting sidings containing two train loads of ash and rubble. These had been left during the afternoon by J37 No.64621 and J36 No.65343, the intention being to work these over the disused Craighead viaduct across the Clyde on the closed

section to Hamilton for filling in the tunnel under the Newton-Hamilton West line, near Burnbank.

While the V1 rounded, the stationmaster was busy selling tickets to enthusiasts for the last departure at 5.45pm, to Jordanhill. The train exploded half a dozen detonators as it left. I travelled back to Shettleston on this service, arriving at 6.02pm, and some twenty minutes later No.69564 arrived from Bothwell with the empty stock of the 5.02pm ex-Hyndland, which it propelled into the sidings at Shettleston Junction. I then got the 6.35pm back to Bothwell (6.09pm from Hyndland), the final service on the branch, consisting of No.69510 with five non-corridors, one of them an ex-Great North of Scotland vehicle. Bothwell was reached punctually at 6.52pm, the loco exploding several detonators as it left the station for Shettleston with the empty stock. It has to be said that, throughout the final hours of the branch, local people showed little or no interest. The line lost its residual goods traffic on 6th June 1961, although the massive viaducts were not dismantled until 1963.

On 23rd June 1960, Fairburn 2-6-4T No.42694 simmers in the terminal platforms at Rutherglen with the 8.35pm train to Balloch, which includes a former LMS triple non-corridor set in its make-up. Note the lengthy footbridge spanning the sprawling nine platform station and, on the extreme left, the platforms on the east side of the triangle. The distinctive Town Hall tower remains a familiar landmark.

A LONG JOURNEY HOME

Switchback, Burma Road - call it what you will – the Caley line round the north eastern outskirts of Glasgow was officially the Possil station to Strathclyde Junction via Balornock Junction route, and also something of a mystery to enthusiasts. It saw only freight trains as a rule, although there were rumours of a short-lived passenger service. Perhaps some of the mystery was a legacy of both World Wars, as troop trains went this way under a cloak of secrecy, while during the 1914-18 conflict, hospital trains were a frightening reminder of the carnage in Flanders. In its last years the line had an unenviable reputation, for certain inhabitants found that by spreading grease on the tracks, trains loaded with whisky or coal could be brought to a stand and plundered.

The western section was sometimes used by special passenger trains, but

The Central Low Level line is seen here on 25th September 1964 in its death throes, with Black Five No.45029 hauling the 4.06pm Coatbridge Central to Dumbarton arriving at deserted and rainswept Parkhead Stadium, a station only too obviously in the last stages of dilapidation. The class A headlamp code was carried, not because the train had any claim to being an express (in fact it called at all but two of the twenty stations en route) but because of the risk to the crew from overhead electrification wires if attaching a lamp to the top bracket on the smokebox door.

Balornock to Rutherglen saw only the very occasional diversion, planned or otherwise, as I found on Saturday 2nd August 1958 when returning from a photographic session on the east coast. The train concerned was the 7.50pm from Thornton Junction to Glasgow Buchanan Street, comprising B1 No.61349 with four corridor coaches, two non-corridors and a couple of vans. Falkirk Grahamston had been left five minutes late at 9.40pm and some brisk running followed, but at 10.06pm we were brought to a stand at Cardowan signal box, the guard eventually intimating that with both lines blocked by the derailment of empty coaches at Stepps carriage sidings, we were to be diverted to Central station.

After some forty minutes, our B1 reversed on the colliery branch and departed light engine. There followed a long silent wait in bright moonlight before Black Five No.45151 came up behind us and coupled up. At 11.35pm we moved off to run wrong line through Garnkirk station to Gartcosh Junction before passing through Coatbridge Central. After a brief stop at Carmyle at midnight we joined the West Coast Main Line at Rutherglen East Junction. However, at Rutherglen we diverged at Dalmarnock Junction and crossed the Clyde, despite the earlier announcement of diversion to Central. At Strathclyde Junction we took the London Road goods line and crossed East End streets lined by darkened tenements, flanges squealing round the curves as we

climbed past Parkhead Forge, over the Queen Street Low Level line, under Edinburgh Road and past Kennyhill goods depot. After the toil up through Blackhill we joined our original route by means of the spur from Balornock Junction to Germiston Junction, then descended through St. Rollox before arriving in Buchanan Street at 12.29am, 2 hours 20 minutes late! I walked home, not too dissatisfied with the evening's events, leaving an irate crowd besieging the stationmaster's office and demanding transport for which, needless to say, no provision had been made.

Right. On the overcast evening of 13th June 1963, 4MT 2-6-0 No.76000 runs into Carmyle station, set amid drab industrial surroundings, with the 4.06pm from Coatbridge Central to Dumbarton. The large signal box in the background was at the junction of the Newton and Coatbridge lines, while the Central Low Level and Rutherglen routes diverged behind the photographer. Passenger trains between Coatbridge and Rutherglen were reinstated during 1993.

Below. In evening sunshine, Fairburn 2-6-4T No.42200 traverses the Newton to Carmyle line with a parcels train from Hamilton on 19th August 1963. The chimneys in the background are those of Hallcraig steelworks, since demolished, while derelict colliery bings form the skyline on the right.

Langloan, on the grimy outskirts of Coatbridge, was notorious for pollution from the surrounding heavy industry, and Fairburn 2-6-4T No.42201 was adding to the smog as it entered the station with the 5.07pm from Balloch to Coatbridge Central on 20th June 1961.

Rebuilt Patriot No 45528 and a Fairburn 2-6-4T go off shed at Polmadie on 12th April 1958. The 4-6-0, a last-minute replacement for Princess Royal No.46203 PRINCESS MARGARET ROSE which had been derailed in the shed yard, was to work the 5.40pm from Glasgow Central to London Euston, a train which took a monumental 11¼ hours.

Evening at Polmadie on 12th April 1958, with 'beetlecrusher' No.56159 and Standard 2-6-4T No 80058 making for the shed, having been coaled up for the next day. Crab No.42883, a Caley 'Jumbo' and a couple of Black 5s await attention on the ash pits.

CHAPTER 7
ON SHED

In the 1950s Glasgow had six principal engine sheds, variously providing motive power for express passenger trains, long distance freight, stopping and suburban passenger services, local goods workings, station pilot and carriage sidings duties, together with yard and dock shunting. Three of them, Polmadie, St Rollox and Dawsholm were established by the Caledonian. Eastfield and Parkhead had North British origins, while Corkerhill was a legacy of the Glasgow & South Western Railway. Outlying depots such as Motherwell, Greenock, Kipps and Ardrossan came under the auspices of the main Glasgow sheds.

Polmadie (66A) alongside the main line near Rutherglen, had an impressive retinue of Pacifics and 4-6-0s for working expresses from Glasgow Central to Carlisle and beyond. It was also responsible for passenger trains to Edinburgh Princes Street, Gourock, Wemyss Bay, Hamilton, Motherwell, Kirkhill, East Kilbride and those on the Cathcart Circle. Goods duties included Paisley-Barrhead workings and General Terminus iron ore trains. A contingent of 0-6-0Ts was maintained for yard shunting. Associated depots were Motherwell (66B), Hamilton (66C) and Greenock Ladyburn and Princes

Pier (66D). St Rollox (65B), alongside the original Garnkirk & Glasgow line at Balornock, worked passenger trains from Buchanan Street to Perth, Aberdeen, Inverness and Oban, as well as a local service to Hamilton. An important responsibility was the provision of motive power for main line freights to the north of Scotland and Carlisle. A number of yard shunters were also allocated here. Dawsholm (65D), hidden away in the Kelvin Valley below Maryhill, was responsible for Central Low Level passenger services from Balloch, Dumbarton and Possil to Rutherglen, Carmyle and other places south east of Glasgow. Heavy mineral traffic from Rothesay Dock to Lanarkshire steelworks was also handled, mainly by Austerity 2-8-0s. There was also a sub-shed at Dumbarton.

Eastfield (65A), occupying a large site alongside the Edinburgh & Glasgow line out of Queen Street, operated passenger services to Edinburgh Waverley via both Falkirk and Bathgate, as well as West Highland trains to Fort William. It was also responsible for main line goods traffic over the former North British system and provided Cowlairs Incline bankers as well as Cadder Yard pilots. The sub-

shed at Stobcross, housing Queen's Dock shunters, closed in 1950. Parkhead (65C), alongside the Airdrie line, worked Queen Street Low Level passenger services to Helensburgh, Balloch, Milngavie, Airdrie, Bridgeton and Springburn. Transfer freights and yard shunting were other responsibilities. Other sheds in the Eastfield group were Kipps (65E), Grangemouth (65F), Yoker (65G and originally Caledonian) which provided Rothesay Dock shunters, Helensburgh (65H) and Balloch (65I). Corkerhill (67A) was the former Glasgow & South Western shed. It stood next to the Paisley Canal line and worked passenger trains to Greenock Princes Pier, Ayr, Largs, Stranraer, Kilmarnock and Carlisle via Dumfries.

By 10th June 1959, the long-standing Caley inhabitants of Dawsholm shed had been joined by strangers in the shape of ex-North British J35 0-6-0 No.64477 and Standard Mogul No.76103. Other foreigners included N15 0-6-2Ts and an N2 0-6-2T. The latter was soon laid aside, but is believed to have visited Balloch, a line from which the class was banned.

Shadows lengthen for Scottish Region steam a year before its demise. This is Eastfield shed on 2nd April 1966, with St Margarets Black 5 No.45477 ready for one of four return specials from Glasgow Queen Street to Edinburgh Waverley following the Scotland v England Football International at Hampden Park. Lurking in the gloom are a dead Standard 2-6-4T and B1 4-6-0 No.61116, which replaced a diesel multiple unit on a Thornton Junction working. The B1 has a self-weighing tender – coaled to capacity, or more!

A number of 0-6-0s and tanks were also based here for local goods and dock shunting. A cluster of substantial houses formed the adjacent railway village. Other sheds in the group were Hurlford (67B), which served Kilmarnock and had sub-sheds in the uplands at Beith and Muirkirk, Ayr (67C) and Ardrossan (67D) on the Clyde coast.

UNSUNG HERO
Parkhead shed, situated in the drab east end of Glasgow and overshadowed by Beardmore's giant Parkhead Forge, provided workaday locomotives for an unglamorous hotchpotch of goods trips, yard shunting and local passenger work. It was generally ignored by locospotters, so perhaps a brief tribute to those who laboured in conditions unacceptable by today's standards of health and safety

to keep engines running and traffic moving will not be out of place. A visit on the overcast evening of Friday 10th July 1959 found the blackened six-road shed (re-roofed after the war but retaining its peculiar castellated end walls) occupied by B1 No.61344, V1 No.67622, V3s Nos.67607, 67614, 67643 and 67675, J37s Nos.64573, 64610 and 64626, and diesel shunters D3532 and D3562. Also present was

Eastfield shed on the evening of 7th May 1959, with K2 No.61787 LOCH QUOICH, J36 No.65315 and Sentinel self-propelled ash crane No.RS 1032/1½. There were two of these machines, delivered in 1929 and 1931 respectively, for use in the Glasgow and Edinburgh areas. They were variously referred to as cranes, wagon stock or departmental locomotives, which puzzled not only enthusiasts but apparently the railway authorities themselves, as the pair changed their running numbers on several occasions over the years. No.RS 1032/1½ (the prefix stood for Rail Steam and 1½ indicated the lifting capacity in tons) was consigned to the scrap heap two months after the photograph was taken.

North Eastern designed, but BR-built, J72 No.69015, said by the leading fitter to be the Parkhead loco requiring least attention!

In the west yard (the shed turntable was close by the entrance) several engines were shrouded in drifting smoke. They were B1 No.61117, much used on football specials and the like since being transferred from Eastfield several years previously, V1 No.67676, V3 No.67612, J35 No.64461, J36 No.65273 and N15 No.69194. Standing outside the east end of the shed were K2 No.61769 (with a fractured injector pipe), K2 No.61772 LOCH LOCHY (which later departed for Bridgeton Central to take over the 10.18pm to Helensburgh from an ailing V3 tank), J35 No.64514, J38 No.65900 off a Thornton turn, and N15 No.69198. A siding known as the 'long lye', leading to the coaling tower at the country end of the shed yard, contained V1s Nos.67629, 67648 and 67655, V3s Nos.67611 and 67681 and N15 No.69165.

Stored in the open, never to run again, were relics from an earlier era in the shape of N2s Nos.69508 and 69563 and C16s Nos.67482 and 67487. Dumped at the back of the shed were N2 No.69507 and C16 No.67500, both optimistically described as 'stored serviceable'. Ominous signs, both of impending dieselisation and the decline in freight traffic, were rusting J35 No.64520 and N15s Nos.69151, 69165 and 69199, laid aside from an allocation already much reduced since the disastrous ASLEF strike of 1955. These derelict locos had been joined by J37

No.64584, which had been used on an excursion from Balloch to Largs earlier in the week but had broken a piston valve, cracked a cylinder and bent a connecting rod while passing Fairlie. The train had been reported running an hour late; possibly excessive speed in an attempt to regain time had caused the failure with a class of loco prone to heating. Black 5 No.44977 of Fort William shed took the return working and the J37 arrived back at Parkhead late that evening hauled by a Black 5 and with a Standard 4MT Mogul attached at the rear. 'Fit for the scrap heap' remarked my informant and, sure enough, No.64584 figured in the next list of withdrawals, only the second member of the class to be condemned.

A total of forty engines had been seen at Parkhead, in contrast to a visit to Polmadie two days previously which had produced no less than 134, ranging from Caley 'Jumbos' to Duchess Pacifics. However, Parkhead had a brief moment of glory when, over the weekend of 17th/18th December 1960, heroic efforts by management and staff ensured sufficient steam locos were available to operate Queen Street Low Level passenger services from Monday 19th, following temporary withdrawal of the 'Blue Trains'. This decision was not officially made until the early hours of Sunday morning, although Parkhead had started putting engines back into steam on Friday afternoon. Electric services resumed on 1st October 1961 and the shed closed four years later. The site is still vacant.

PARKHEAD (65C)
Allocation 1950
Class 5MT 4-6-0
44791
Class K2 2-6-0
61772 LOCH LOCHY
Class J37 0-6-0
64548, 64559, 64563, 64573, 64584, 64609, 64610, 64621, 64626
Class J36 0-6-0
65274, 65283, 65298, 65324, 65335
Class C15 4-4-2T
67454, 67470, 67477, 67480
Class C16 4-4-2T
67487
Class V1/V3 ex-LNE Gresley 2-6-2T
67604, 67611, 67612, 67619, 67621, 67622, 67623, 67626, 67628, 67633, 67643, 67648, 67655, 67661, 67662, 67676, 67678, 67681
Class J69 0-6-0T
68503, 68567
Class N15 0-6-2T
69143, 69151, 69157, 69161, 69171, 69190, 69193, 69194, 69195, 69198, 69199, 69209, 69210, 69212, 69213, 69214, 69217
Class N2 0-6-2T
69500, 69507, 69510, 69511, 69514, 69553, 69562, 69564, 69565, 69595

PARKHEAD
Allocation 1959
Class B1 4-6-0
61067, 61117, 61333, 61344, 61404
Class K2 2-6-0
61769, 61772 LOCH LOCHY
Class J35 0-6-0
64461, 64520
Class J37 0-6-0
64559, 64563, 64573, 64584, 64609,

Kipps shed was sited at the east end of Coatbridge, where a short branch from the pioneering Monkland & Kirkintilloch Railway met the Ballochney Railway and the later North British line from Bathgate. In BR days it housed some forty-five locomotives, predominantly freight, of classes J35, J36, J37, J83, J88, N15 and Y9, together with several N2s and V3s for passenger work. On 30th April 1960 two of the shunters, J88 No.68343 and Y9 No.68110 stood at the coaling plant in light steam before their fires were dropped for the weekend. Both locos are fitted with dumb buffers for working sharply curved sidings.

V3 2-6-2T No.67662 takes water at Clydebank East on 12th September 1959, prior to working the last train before closure, the 8.18pm to Airdrie. All the paraphernalia of the steam railway is here, but the infrastructure for electric working on the nearby line through Clydebank Central is already in situ. There was no place in the new order for the small terminus, which at one time boasted a through service to Edinburgh Waverley via Bathgate.

64621, 64626
Class J36 0-6-0
65211, 65273, 65295
Class C16 4-4-2T
67482, 67487, 67500
Class V1/V3 2-6-2T
67607, 67608, 67611, 67612, 67621, 67623, 67626, 67629, 67630, 67633, 67643, 67648, 67650, 67655, 67661, 67662, 67675, 67676, 67678, 67679, 67681
Class J72 0-6-0T
69015
Class N15 0-6-2T
69161, 69165, 69166, 69190, 69198, 69199, 69209, 69213
Class N2 0-6-2T
69507, 69508, 69509, 69563
Diesel Shunter
D3212, D3213, D3214, D3277, D3410, D3562

LIFE IN THE VILLAGE

In 1895-96, the Glasgow & South Western Railway was engaged in building a large locomotive depot, largely intended to replace the awkwardly sited facilities at St Enoch. To the design of William Melville, the company's Chief Civil Engineer, the new shed was being erected at Corkerhill on the Paisley Canal line, which had opened during the summer of 1885. It lay 4¼ miles from the city centre, adjoining Pollok Estate in open country dotted with a few small coal pits. The new shed was to have an allocation of seventy or more locos, so a 'Model

Railway Village' (to quote Company Chairman and shipyard magnate, Patrick Tennant Caird) was erected at a cost of £70,000 to house the necessary staff. Standing alongside the depot, the village eventually comprised 136 houses in twelve yellow brick two-storey blocks. Some had crow-stepped gables, the remainder featuring mock Tudor half-timbering. Accommodation for the population of around 700 consisted of one, two or three rooms with a kitchen and toilet. Annual rents ranged from £8 to £18 and rates varied from 15 shillings to 17 shillings (75p to 85p!).

An Institute, presided over by an elected committee, provided facilities for social and religious meetings, together with a library, reading and recreation rooms, and a 'suite of baths of the most modern description' (remembered for their enormous size and copious supply of boiling water). There was also a general store. Thrift, Rent and Doctor's Clubs and an Ambulance Association were established and a Flower Show became an annual event. A private station, little more than a halt with small timber buildings, opened on 1st December 1896 to serve both 'the loco' and village. Each tenant and members of his family could purchase, for an annual payment of five shillings (25p), a season ticket for travel into Glasgow. The first residents moved in during 1897, although official opening of the village did not take place until the spring of 1900. Similar G&SW

facilities known as 'The Blocks' were provided at Hurlford depot on the outskirts of Kilmarnock, served by Barleith Halt on the Darvel branch.

With the coming of the LMS in 1923, Corkerhill appeared in the public timetable for the first time, initially as a halt ('no heavy luggage dealt with'). Under British Railways, it was rebuilt during 1954, but closed along with the Canal line in 1983. However, in an astonishing and costly about-turn by Strathclyde PTE, the line was reopened seven years later. Meanwhile, Corkerhill depot had become the home of electric and diesel multiple units. Sadly, the railway village had ceased to exist when the few remaining inhabitants moved out during 1970; the site was then taken over for council housing.

Those brought up in the village during the 1930s have memories of a happy and close-knit community, vibrant with the coming and going of men on shift work. Milk, fruit, vegetables and coal were delivered by horse-drawn carts along the unmade road, although Corporation buses serving the new Mosspark housing scheme were bringing the shops in Paisley Road within reach. There was the ritual of washday at the communal wash house, but great was the dismay when a change of wind sent smoke across the drying green from serried ranks of locomotives in the shed yard. On summer evenings, village children played in the bluebell woods or 'helped' the local farmer with haymaking, while their elders sunned themselves and talked of locomotives and gardening. In winter, there were visits to Glasgow cinemas, sometimes leaving the train at Cumberland Street station for the large *Coliseum* and *New Bedford* in Eglinton Street, the former showing the first talking picture in the city in 1929.

Electricity eventually replaced gas lighting in the village, but coal fires remained. However, any member of staff caught purloining coal from a locomotive or the coaling plant faced instant dismissal. Some of the younger men lodged in the village with widows, an arrangement of mutual benefit as there were no pensions as such, and *ex-gratia* retirement payments (main line drivers received ten shillings a week, lower grades being pro-rata) ceased upon the death of the recipient.

No longer were infant classes held in the Institute, younger children having to walk to the new Mosspark Primary School. Those at secondary school travelled by train to Shields Road station. The railway doctor had his residence at Shields Road and when his services were required in the village outside normal train times, a light engine was despatched to pick him up! For village residents, a season ticket to Glasgow was still priced at five shillings in the 1930s and for an additional half crown, Paisley would be included. A final memory is of the cacophony of sound which greeted the New Year. Caley whistles, overwhelming the few Sou'West ones, mingled with new-fangled Stanier hooters to drown out the sound of ships' sirens from the Clyde.

CORKERHILL (67A)
Allocation 1950
Class 2P 4-4-0
40594, 40595, 40596, 40598, 40599, 40604, 40620, 40621, 40627, 40636, 40637, 40641, 40642, 40649, 40651
Class 4P 4-4-0
40905, 40906, 40909, 40914, 40915, 40919
Class 4MT 2-6-4T
42122, 42123, 42124, 42190, 42191, 42192, 42193, 42194, 42195, 42196, 42197
Class 5MT 2-6-0
42911, 42914, 42916, 42917
Class 4F 0-6-0
43899, 44159, 44198, 44329
Class 5MT 4-6-0
44706, 44968, 45047, 45049, 45163, 45168, 45174, 45194, 45251, 45489, 45490, 45491
Jubilee 4-6-0
45560 PRINCE EDWARD ISLAND, 45576 BOMBAY, 45643 RODNEY, 45645 COLLINGWOOD, 45646 NAPIER, 45693 AGAMEMNON
Class 3F 0-6-0T
47329
Class 2P 0-4-4T
55135, 55140, 55143, 55182, 55206, 55211, 55219, 55225, 55235, 55266, 55269
Class 3F 0-6-0T
56249, 56329, 56350, 56361, 56369
Class 2F 0-6-0
57241, 57249, 57255, 57266, 57300, 57309, 57359
Class 3F 0-6-0
57560, 57562, 57566, 57575, 57580, 57589, 57596, 57695, 57698

CORKERHILL
Allocation 1959
Class 2P 4-4-0
40594, 40596, 40598, 40599, 40620, 40621, 40627, 40636, 40637, 40641, 40642, 40649
Class 4MT 2-6-4T
42122, 42123, 42190, 42191, 42193, 42229, 42238, 42240, 42247
Class 4F 0-6-0
43899, 43996, 44001, 44198, 44319
Class 5MT 4-6-0
44706, 44791, 45007, 45160, 45161, 45194, 45251, 45362, 45489, 45490
Jubilee 4-6-0
45621 NORTHERN RHODESIA, 45665 LORD RUTHERFORD OF NELSON, 45677 BEATTY, 45687 NEPTUNE, 45693 AGAMEMNON, 45707 VALIANT, 45711 COURAGEOUS, 45720 INDOMITABLE
Class 3F 0-6-0T
47329
Class 2P 0-4-4T
55206, 55219, 55225, 55235, 55266
Class 2F 0-6-0T
56156
Class 3F 0-6-0T
56279, 56361, 56364
Class 2F 0-6-0
57241, 57249, 57300, 57359
Class 5 4-6-0
73079, 73100, 73101, 73102, 73103, 73104, 73121, 73122, 73123, 73124
Class 4MT 2-6-0
76090, 76091, 76092, 76093, 76094, 76095, 76096, 76097, 76098, 76099
Class 4MT 2-6-4T
80000, 80008, 80009, 80024, 80025, 80127, 80128

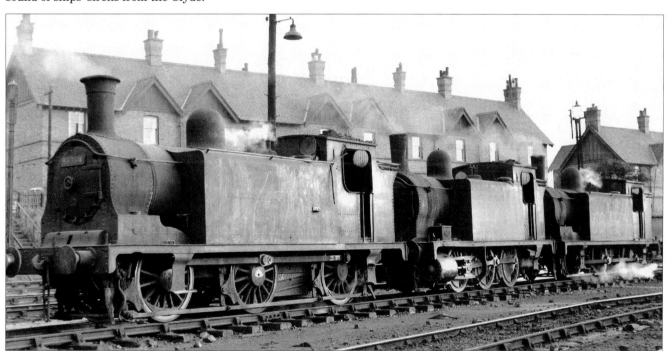

The day's shunting is done and three work-worn Caley 0-6-0Ts line up for disposal at Corkerhill shed on the evening of 22nd July 1959. Former Glasgow & South Western housing in the railway village forms a backdrop. Nos.56364 and 56279, BR class 3F, were the Caledonian Railway's McIntosh-designed standard shunting tank, this pair dating from 1916 and 1905 respectively. No.56156, with its short wheelbase intended for sharply curved dock lines, was also a McIntosh design, although built in 1915 under the Pickersgill regime. The nickname 'beetlecrusher' for the dock shunters was strictly unofficial! Stovepipe chimneys had begun to be fitted at St Rollox Works at the end of World War 2, for what reason has never been precisely defined. They did nothing to enhance the appearance of the locos so treated.

Standard 2-6-4T No.80118 calls at neat little Thorntonhall station on 17th July 1964 with the 8.00am from East Kilbride to Glasgow St Enoch. Although Castlemilk, one of the city's more infamous housing schemes, sprawled over the hills less than three miles to the north, Thorntonhall was decidedly sylvan. In fact just to the west, North Hill of Dripps overlooked the waterfalls of White Cart Water where it tumbled down from the bleak moors of Laird's Seat.

A few loungers look on as a Swindon built Inter-City diesel multiple unit forming the 4.00pm from Edinburgh Waverley to Glasgow Queen Street speeds through Garrowhill Halt on 26th September 1958, diverted via Bathgate from its normal route through Falkirk High because of a derailment. The grim backdrop, reminiscent of East German workers' flats, was only too typical of Glasgow's post-war housing.

CHAPTER 8
TRANSITION

At the beginning of 1957, steam still monopolised local and long distance passenger and goods services on Glasgow's railways. Apart from a few yard shunters and visits by the main-line pair 10000 and 10001, diesel traction had been virtually unknown thus far. However, the successful introduction of diesel multiple units in West Yorkshire during 1954 and the range of diesel locomotives envisaged by the 1955 Modernisation Plan meant that this situation was bound to change drastically. On 7th January 1957, Swindon-built Inter-City units replaced steam on Glasgow Queen Street-Edinburgh Waverley expresses and some suburban services were dieselised the following year. The big English Electric Type 4 diesels appeared on West Coast expresses shortly afterwards, although they were barely a match for a Polmadie Pacific in fine fettle. North British Type 2s became a familiar sight at Buchanan Street from 1960, but they were very prone to failure and a sad swansong for the once-proud Glasgow locomotive builder. Frankly, the introduction of diesel traction was rather a hotchpotch, to the extent that prior to withdrawal in 1964, Central Low Level services were worked by a mixture of Cravens and Metro-Cammell diesel multiple units, English Electric Type 1s, Clayton Type 1s and steam!

Electrification was a different matter. Once the overhead equipment, colour light signalling, power supply and other expensive items were in place, services were transformed overnight. Undoubtedly the most famous electrification project in Glasgow concerned the North Side 'Blue Trains' from Helensburgh, Balloch and Milngavie to Springburn, Bridgeton and Airdrie via Queen Street Low Level during 1960. The official Scottish Region publication by George Blake to celebrate the occasion began as follows:-
'Out of a cutting above the River Clyde and into the sunshine there flashes a train at speed. Its coaches are painted the bright blue of the kingfisher, gay against the softer greens and browns of the fields, and its windows, almost unbroken in length, flash cheerfully. An old man on a chair at a cottage door on the hillside looks down to see that the three coaches rippling along so fast and so purposefully do so as by dark magic; vaguely he misses the smoke and steam, the glowing fires and heaped coals of the engines of his young manhood.

At least, he has lived long enough to see the electric train come to Scotland.'

Unfortunately, serious electrical faults which caused explosions on some of the trains led to the withdrawal of the new units and steam made an heroic, albeit temporary, return. The South Side electrification, involving the Cathcart Circle, Neilston and Kirkhill lines, was inaugurated during 1962, followed by the Gourock and Wemyss Bay routes in 1967 and the Ayr line in 1986. Steam finished in 1967 and West Coast main line electric services reached Glasgow Central during 1974.

TWILIGHT OF STEAM
The spring of 1964 saw us taking up

With diesel traction still something of a novelty, a Cravens twin is the centre of attention at Kelvin Hall station (formerly Partick Central) on 5th September 1959 while operating a shuttle service from Central Low Level for the Scottish Industries Exhibition at Kelvin Hall. The return fare for the four minute journey was eightpence (3½p) and the set ran empty from Central Low Level to Bridgeton Cross for rounding. Kelvin Hall station was specially decorated for the event and received temporary electric lighting.

The Caledonian suburban line from Paisley to Barrhead was seen off, even before it opened, by the electric tram. Indeed, apart from a solitary railtour, no fare paying passengers were ever carried. Freight, however, did produce some revenue and included products from the Pressed Steel Works at Linwood, in this instance a new high-density multiple unit leaving for the Western Region on 23rd May 1960. Other Pressed Steel products included the original Glasgow Blue Trains.

residence at Thorntonhall, a surprisingly rural retreat, yet only some eight miles from Glasgow city centre and thus within range of the travel concessions granted to BR staff. Situated on the single line section of the East Kilbride branch, the station had been served by diesel multiple units since 1959 (at the same time, trains had been transferred from Central to St Enoch). Nevertheless, a pair of peak period trains in each direction remained loco-hauled and, until their disappearance in 1966, gave me a last opportunity of commuting behind steam. Thereafter, journeys into the city were by dmu and, since retirement and a return to Glasgow itself, by electric multiple units on the Neilston branch. The steam trains in question, running Mondays to Fridays, were the 8.00am and 8.15am from East Kilbride and the 5.08pm and 5.33pm from St Enoch (the 24-hour clock was not used until mid-1965). The first of the morning trains and the second of the evening pair were worked by Polmadie shed, while the

Southern Region main line diesels Nos.10201 and 10202, built at Ashford Works in 1951 and classified 6P/5F, pass Uddingston Junction with the down 'Royal Scot' (10.00am London Euston to Glasgow Central) on 27th July 1957. The Bellshill line comes in from the left, while the former North British branch from Shettleston to Bothwell and Hamilton crosses the bridge in the middle distance.

Diverted from Central station because of on-going resignalling work and track rationalisation for the forthcoming South Side suburban electrification scheme, English Electric Type 4 No.D334 leaves platform 5 of Buchanan Street at 6.45pm on Sunday 28th May 1961 with the up West Coast postal. D332 worked the 6.50pm to Euston and a V2 2-6-2 the 7.15pm for Dundee. In the background, Buchanan Street goods depot was in decline and closed the following year.

others had Corkerhill engines and men. The locos, coupled together, went up in the early morning to collect the six coach non-corridor sets which had been stabled overnight beyond East Kilbride station on a siding formed by the surviving portion of the line to Blantyre and Hamilton. Surprisingly, the carriages suffered very little vandalism, despite their isolated position. After the stock was deposited in the evening, the two engines made a high speed descent of the branch, going their separate ways at Strathbungo Junction. However, at summer weekends the empty stock was frequently brought back on Friday evening for Clyde Coast reliefs and returned on Saturday evening.

The Corkerhill turns were almost invariably worked by Standard 2-6-4Ts, but Polmadie provided plenty of variety with Stanier and Standard 5MT 4-6-0s, 4MT Moguls and Fairburn 2-6-4Ts. Occasionally, Type 1 or Type 2 diesels appeared and Claytons were tried – but not for long, as they were extremely slow and noisy on the climb to East Kilbride and, in any case, did not have any means of train heating. Timekeeping, while perhaps not of the best (for a seven week period in 1964 the 5.33pm was unable to achieve a single punctual arrival at Thorntonhall) could be described as reasonable. But there were occasional incidents, seemingly inseparable from

commuting. Perhaps the worst of these came with a freezing fog on 25th January 1965, when a combined 5.33pm/5.54pm from St Enoch worked by Corkerhill 2-6-4T No.80112 eventually got me home 65 minutes late at 7.03pm. On 1st March 1965, there were apologies for an unspecified 'failure' and No.80063 was commandeered from empty stock, but had to take water prior to working the 5.33pm. Polmadie 2-6-4T No.42199 belatedly (and unfortunately, as it turned out) arrived and was substituted. We set off at 5.55pm, but after a five-minute 'blow-up' at Thornliebank in driving snow, the engine expired on arrival at Giffnock and summoned up just enough energy to move the stock into the sidings, over half an hour after the train should have left for East Kilbride.

Giffnock was the scene of another unfortunate incident, on 8th November 1965, when No.80130 failed with a defective boiler washout plug while working the 08.00 to St Enoch, resulting in the fire having to be dropped. With admirable promptness, Clayton No.D8547 arrived from Pollokshaws Yard to shunt the Standard tank, shrouded in steam, out of the way. The diesel took over the train, which continued only 24 minutes late. On 6th December the 08.00 was a Central SMT double deck bus as, owing to frozen

points, no trains had been able to reach East Kilbride. The last of a catalogue of misfortunes came on 22nd February 1966 when No.80000 on the 17.08 came to a stand with vacuum failure shortly after leaving St Enoch. Some twenty minutes later, D8537 arrived from High Street yard and the train resumed its journey, hauled by steam but with the diesel providing braking power attached to the rear. Meanwhile, on the rainy evening of 19th November 1965, I had achieved my target for the year of 10,000 miles of steam travel in the Scottish Region, when No.76103 passed Gorbals Junction with the 17.33.

Despite the rundown of steam, the summer of 1965 had brought an event unusual in my experience of commuting, when No.80001 worked the 8.00am for two weeks without a break, reappearing in early August and again in September, for five days in succession. Nos.80116 and 80120 were also very consistent performers. By now, ex-works locos were to be seen running in on the 17.33, including Black Fives Nos.44838 (8A Edge Hill) and 45403 (6A Chester). On 24th January 1966, Standard class 4MT 4-6-0 No.75010 (6A), of a type never allocated to the Scottish Region, was used for both the 08.00 and 17.33. It proved something of a disaster on the evening train, which left five minutes late because of the non-availability of

To the bemusement of the ladies with the push-chair awaiting a Cathcart Inner Circle train, a pair of class 50s (Nos.440 and 408) roar through Shawlands station with the 17.25 Glasgow Central to Liverpool and Manchester, diverted from the main line because of electrification work. The date is 7th April 1973.

stock. A combination of signal checks and excessive slipping on rails made greasy by a thick wet mist saw a 23 minute late arrival at Thorntonhall. Things were not much better on the 27th, when an eleven minutes late arrival was recorded. However, by 4th February Polmadie had got to grips with this strange machine and, despite a train crammed to capacity because of a local bus strike and a 1½ minute late departure, No.75010 made a triumphal entry into East Kilbride punctually at 18.10. Here, commuters poured from every compartment and surged along the

On 14th May 1959, K4 2-6-0 No.61995 CAMERON OF LOCHIEL from Eastfield shed is in charge of a concreting train at work on the Clydebank line in connection with the North Side electrification. The K4s had been introduced in 1937/38 to obviate double heading on the West Highland line, but by the mid-1950s they were relegated to odd jobs from Eastfield and finished their days in Fife during 1961, working from Thornton shed.

Following a series of Blue Train failures, prior to them entering service, four green-liveried 'Tilbury' sets were borrowed for test running and driver training. The quartet, Nos.205, 258, 260 and 261, are seen here at Hyndland Depot on 16th January 1960 shortly before they returned south of the border.

gas-lit platform, a scene reminiscent of a bygone era.

With reversion of East Kilbride trains to Central station on 18th April 1966, a move associated with the forthcoming closure of St Enoch, steam working finished on Friday 15th April. On this overcast evening, with an east wind bringing flurries of snow, I made my last journey with the 17.33. It was worked by Polmadie's rusting Standard tank No.80121 which laboured up the branch and reached East Kilbride five minutes late. The stock, no longer required, was being worked away to South Side carriage sidings. Corkerhill's 4MT tank No.80046 was waiting in the loop to depart with coaches off the 17.08 and No.80121 followed later with its own train. The latter cleared Busby Junction at approximately 18.40, bringing to an end, as the local paper put it 'one hundred years of steam locomotion on the Busby Railway.'

THE VERY END
The spring of 1967 brought an unwelcome memo to my desk. 'With improved availability ... it is proposed to substitute, as from 1st May 1967, DMU stock ... and thereby eliminate steam engine working on suburban services in the Glasgow Division.' This effectively heralded the end of steam passenger operations within the Scottish Region, although occasional

forays by Carlisle Kingmoor locos were to continue until the end of the year. At Central station on the last morning (Friday 28th April), Black Five No.44699 of Corkerhill shed took out the 06.55 to Hillington West, the train then running empty to Cart Junction for rounding before forming the 07.55 from Paisley Canal back to Glasgow. Standard tank No.80004 worked the 07.19 from Central to Renfrew Fulbar Street, then took the stock to Smithy Lye. However, English Electric type 1 diesel No.D8124 was used for the 08.23 to Gourock, normally a steam turn.

A visit to Polmadie shed at lunchtime revealed Fairburn 2-6-4T No.42274 booked light engine to Gourock to work the 17.03 passenger to Glasgow and Standard 5MT No.73060 rostered for the 16.54 from Central to Gourock. Disappointingly, type 1 No.D8124 was shown for the 15.57 to Gourock and type 2 No.D5363 for the 16.22 from Bishopton. Also in steam were three carriage pilots, Black Five No.44796 and Standard 2-6-4Ts Nos.80116 and 80120, together with Britannia No.70012 (formerly JOHN OF GAUNT) and Standard Five No.73059. In the event, the 16.54 (by which I travelled to Bishopton) was diesel-hauled by No.D8031 and there were disquieting rumours of a ban on steam, following a flashover involving the overhead wires in Bishopton tunnel.

Whatever the truth of this, the presence of No.42274 at Gourock seems to have been overlooked and a distant whistle heralded its approach with the 17.03. This consisted of four BR Standard non-corridors and the train departed punctually at 17.43 in bright sunshine. It called at Paisley St James, lost two minutes at Paisley Gilmour Street with 'station duties' (a barrow load of mail), touched 62mph passing Cardonald, got a signal check at Ibrox, and ran into platform 12 of Central station slightly before the booked arrival time of 18.07. Ten minutes later the stock was propelled out for Smithy Lye to rousing exhaust from No.42274.

Next day, the carriage pilots (Nos.44796 and 80116) were in steam for the last time, as were the Beattock bankers (Nos.76104, 45359 and 45423) and *The Scotsman* newspaper noted that 'huffing, puffing steam engines, all boiler and bombast, have disappeared from Scotland'. Although almost completely ignored by railway staff and enthusiasts alike, this was the end of an era which had started 136 years previously with the formal opening of the Garnkirk & Glasgow Railway on 27th September 1831. A small memento in my keeping is the smokebox number plate from No.44699, which I purchased for the princely sum of £1.

A new Blue Train comes off the Milngavie branch at Westerton Junction on 22nd March 1960 during test running. These three-car sets were well ahead of their time in both exterior and interior design. Attention to detail included green and red seating in the centre vehicles, contrasting with brown, cream and black striped moquette in the outer coaches.

The first eastbound Blue Train was the 12.04pm from Drumry to Airdrie on 5th November 1960. This is it calling at the new Hyndland station, the first service to do so. These through platforms replaced the original terminus at the end of a branch.

A westbound Blue Train, the 17.48 from Airdrie to Helensburgh, passes the ex-North British signal box at Shettleston Junction on 6th September 1968. The former Hamilton branch joined the Airdrie line here and there were also marshalling sidings and an engineer's yard in days gone by, with signal boxes at Shettleston East and West.

And finally... Springburn station on 25th July 1968 with the 13.41 electric train for Queen Street Low Level and Milngavie, providing a connection with the diesel railcar from Cumbernauld. This arrangement was made necessary by the closure of Buchanan Street station and consequent withdrawal of through trains serving Cumbernauld. The former North British Locomotive Co. Hyde Park Works is on the right, facing the similarly derelict Atlas Works beyond the platforms. The notorious Red Road flats at Balornock form a grim sight in the left background. The Cumbernauld shuttle has been replaced by through running to and from Queen Street High Level via the new Cowlairs chord line.

Despite modernisation, electrification and the passage of time, one or two stations on the Glasgow railway network continued to exude character from a bygone era. The proud and exquisite Caledonian building at Maxwell Park dominated an original Blue Train, by then in Strathclyde orange and black livery, as it paused during a Cathcart Outer Circle working on the evening of 22nd April 1991. Photograph Paul Anderson.